The Librarian's Guide to
MICRO
PUBLISHING

The Librarian's Guide to
MICRO PUBLISHING

Helping Patrons and Communities Use Free and Low-Cost Publishing Tools to Tell Their Stories

Walt Crawford

Information Today, Inc.
Medford, New Jersey

First printing, 2012

The Librarian's Guide to Micropublishing: Helping Patrons and Communities Use Free and Low-Cost Publishing Tools to Tell Their Stories

Library of Congress Cataloging-in-Publication Data

Crawford, Walt.
    The librarian's guide to micropublishing : helping patrons and communities use free and low-cost publishing tools to tell their stories / Walt Crawford.
       pages cm
    Includes bibliographical references and index.
    ISBN 978-1-57387-430-4
1. Libraries and publishing. 2. On-demand publications. 3. Libraries--Publishing--Computer programs. 4. Desktop publishing. I. Title.
    Z716.6C73 2012
    070.5'94--dc23

                                                                                    2011044882

Perfect-bound paperback ISBN: 978-1-57387-430-4
Lulu "proof of concept" hardbound ISBN: 978-1-57387-451-9

President and CEO: Thomas H. Hogan, Sr.
Editor-in-Chief and Publisher: John B. Bryans
VP Graphics and Production: M. Heide Dengler
Managing Editor: Amy M. Reeve
Editorial Assistant: Brandi Scardilli
Cover Designer: Lisa Conroy

www.infotoday.com

Contents

About the Website
waltcrawford.name/lgm

This book has an accompanying website, *Librarian's Guide to Micropublishing Notes and Links*, at waltcrawford.name/lgm.

The website contains links to the templates discussed in this book (bk6pv.dotx, bp6pvex.dotx, the .dot versions of those templates, and the bk6lb.ott template for LibreOffice) and to resources mentioned in the book. It also links to a page providing basic information for associations that might wish to engage me for a speech or workshop on micropublishing.

The website may be enriched (either before or after this book appears in print) with additional templates, links, and resources, such as free or very inexpensive ways to convert Microsoft Word-formatted books to EPUB and Kindle formats (if I discover and test such ways) and other useful resources for micropublishers.

My personal website, waltcrawford.name, will also have a link to *Librarian's Guide to Micropublishing Notes and Links*. You may also find occasional items related to micropublishing in my blog (*Walt at Random*, walt.lishost.org) or my ejournal (*Cites & Insights*, citesandinsights.info).

1
Libraries and Micropublishing

You have genealogy enthusiasts who want to publish their family histories, but the results might only be interesting to a dozen family members. At least 1 percent of your patrons, probably more, have family histories or genealogies they'd like to see in print form. Your library can help.

Beyond formal family histories and genealogies, more and more of your patrons may be gathering remembrances worth keeping and sharing: great-great-great-grandmother's narrative of crossing the plains to California or Utah. Great-great grandfather's story of growing up a slave and becoming a trusted member of the community, or mother's memories of the Civil Rights Movement. Grandfather's story of war, sacrifice, and change in the first half of the 20th century. Your generation's stories of growing up with technology, being in garage bands, coping with the conflicts between social networks and privacy. Some of these are powerful family and community narratives worth preserving in book form. Your library can help.

Your community is surrounded by parks and wilderness preserves with scores of hiking trails—and more hiking and interesting walking routes in the urban non-wilderness. Members of a local hiking group have gathered comments on the most interesting (and least known) trails, including drawings and information to share those trails with other hikers. Chances are nobody outside your community and neighboring communities will care, but those within your community might find this a great resource. Your library can help.

A group of teens in your community forms a writing club to inspire one another's creativity and review one another's prose and poetry. At the end of the first year, they have a collection of the best works they'd love to have bound copies of—and so would their parents. Your library can help.

Local historians have produced a first-rate history of your community, but your community's not big enough to attract a traditional publisher, given that the history might only attract 20, 30, or 300 readers. Your library can help.

Your academic library serves as the sponsoring agency for one or more open access scholarly journals using Open Journal Systems or other open source software and publishing articles on the web as PDFs, perhaps totaling two dozen papers and 400 pages for a journal's annual volume. You believe a handful of libraries and a handful of authors would love to have proper print volumes of the journal, but there's no way to justify a big print run. Your library can help.

You can probably think of hundreds of other examples, cases where there are stories to be told within your communities, stories worth preserving that won't attract a big publisher and that don't justify spending thousands of dollars for a big press run. Chances are, at least one out of five of your community members has a potential book in them—and at least a quarter of those potential books would be worth having for some number of readers. Your library can help.

Consider an extreme case. Someone in your community wants to gather some family stories or put together some advice—and only wants one copy, a single hardback volume to be handed down to the next generation. Your library can help.

Or another extreme: A person or group in your community is an expert in a narrow field, one so narrow that his or her expertise *might* only be useful for two dozen others in the world—but it might turn out to be attractive to two thousand or more. Your library can help.

And it won't cost your library a dime—other than this book, possibly in multiple copies. Your library can enhance your community and increase the library's role in that community by helping patrons and groups of patrons tell their stories using free and low-cost tools.

Stories come in all lengths and flavors and include fiction and nonfiction. We use stories to share wisdom and ideas as well as experiences. Everybody in your community has stories to share; many people in every community have stories that others can benefit from.

Everybody has knowledge others can learn from, and lifelong learning is one of the primary missions of public libraries. Some of that knowledge is and remains local; some begins at a local level and should be shared more broadly.

People also love to share experiences—living vicariously but also gaining background for future adventures. Your library may already host travel presentations by community members. Cumulated experiences make great books, and micropublishing can make those books real. They can also serve our natural tendency to be interested in ourselves and those around us; local experience carries special flavor. Micropublishing strengthens a community by sharing its stories.

Every public library—from volunteer-run libraries serving 200 people to well-funded systems serving millions—can use micropublishing effectively, as facilitator, micropublisher, or both. So can many academic libraries, especially smaller ones in colleges and universities without a university press.

This book will show you how micropublishing works, cover the steps of book publishing and how micropublishing affects those steps, identify the tools you need to proceed (tools you and your patrons probably already own), and show you and your community members how to get from "good enough" micropublished books to ones that look almost as good as anything from the biggest trade publishers.

Defining Micropublishing

What is micropublishing?

Historically, the term refers to publishing in microform, on microfiche, reel microfilm, or microcard. Recently, the term has been used for a variety of niche publishing techniques. Increasingly, however, the word is being used as defined here:

> **Micropublishing uses print on demand fulfillment services to publish books that may serve niches from one to 500 copies, by producing books individually as they are needed.**

In the past, I've used POD—publish on demand—for what this book calls micropublishing. But the accepted and broadest expansion of POD is *print* on demand. Many publishers use Lightning Source (www.lightningsource.com, a division of the Ingram Content Group),

BookSurge (www.booksurge.com, a division of Amazon), or Replica Books (www.unlimitedpublishing.com/bt, a division of Baker & Taylor) to keep books alive by producing a few copies as needed, rather than the thousands required for an economical press run using traditional techniques. For that matter, some academic publishers and smaller publishers use POD for *all* book production. At this point, tens of millions of books each year are produced through print on demand; it's an established technology.

Given the ambiguity of POD and given that publish on demand uses print on demand techniques, it makes sense to adopt a different term: micropublishing.

A key element of the definition above is "print on demand fulfillment services." For the purposes of this book, that means Lulu and CreateSpace, two companies that handle the entire back end of publishing (printing, binding, order taking, money handling, and shipping) with no up-front charges except for optional added services. These companies may very well use Lightning Source or BookSurge to print the books. (Since CreateSpace is a division of Amazon, it's fair to assume it uses BookSurge as a printing partner. Lulu has printing partners in several dozen countries.) It's quite possible that we'll see a future in which some bookstores and libraries have self-contained book production devices, such as the Espresso Book Machine, with links that make it feasible for micropublished books to be produced on site.

Micropublished books may not carry a formal imprint name or may carry a name created for the purposes of a single book—or the author's name as publisher. Micropublished books may or may not have ISBNs or jacket prices. Some micropublished books may not have formal prices at all: It's quite plausible for a micropublished book never to enter any formal sales channel, produced only for use by a family or group or for promotional purposes. What micropublished books have in common is that they're produced in very small numbers.

Why Libraries Should Be Involved in Micropublishing

Why micropublish? To produce niche books, books that are not expected to sell many copies. To avoid the complexities and overhead of becoming a small publisher, including costs and accounting issues of sales and fulfillment. To test the waters for a new concept that might or might not have broad appeal. And to do any or all of these with little or no capital investment.

Why libraries? Because it's a great fit with your mission and a new niche that should improve your community standing.

Public libraries serve lifelong learning and serve to collect, organize, and preserve the stories that make up our civilization. Micropublishing adds new local voices to that set of stories.

Most public libraries serve as community centers with a particular focus on the community's literary and learning needs and desires. Many public libraries have writing groups, book clubs, and other story-oriented groups. These groups can form natural support groups for micropublishers and, along with teen groups and other groups that meet as part of library programming or within library spaces, can be great sources for new micropublished works.

Nearly all public libraries have public access computers with most or all of the software needed for micropublishing—and with broadband access to support micropublishing's uploading requirements. When the library adds explicit support for micropublishing, it becomes a creation center, a place where people make their stories formal and permanent.

In short, public libraries already gather the resources to make micropublishing work well and to benefit from its possibilities. It's a safe bet that there are people within your library community—no matter how small—who would not only benefit from micropublishing but would add worthwhile new voices. Who better than the library to facilitate that process?

Academic libraries may increasingly be involved in publishing to assist faculty and (in some cases) students or to take over functions that might otherwise be handled by university presses. With the growth of open access journals, especially in smaller areas in the humanities and social sciences, academic libraries can be natural centers for new journals. In the case of journals, micropublishing can provide an extension of ejournals to print form with very little effort and no new costs for the library. In the case of monographs, micropublishing can reduce the capital investment required for publication and make it feasible to do niche monographs. At least one academic library already uses micropublishing to support a virtual university press; more will follow.

Making the Most of Micropublishing

How should your library promote micropublishing to make it an effective service that improves the community and your library's standing?

For most public libraries, the first answer is on your website as a tab or a link: genealogy. Your library probably serves genealogical researchers and family history enthusiasts. Contact the local genealogy society or the family historians who use your library; let them know about micropublishing and this book. Almost certainly, there are two groups of people who will use micropublishing and benefit from it: people doing family histories for the first time, and people who have existing family histories, frequently prepared as typescripts or spiral-bound photocopies, that they'd like to update and turn into good-looking, lasting books.

The next major focus overlaps with the first: local history. Does your library have a local history room or collection? Is there a local history group? Micropublishing offers a way to produce better local histories and make them more usable.

Does your library have special collections—specifically documents that aren't suitable for circulation but matter to your community and your patrons? If you have appropriate rights or documents old enough to be in the public domain, you might consider micropublishing—combining documents into books that may be of special interest to those in your community. Such books might even be modest fundraisers for the library.

If your library already has writing groups, such groups will find micropublishing useful. Let them know about this book. If your library is expanding its work to foster community creativity, micropublishing is a natural part of such work.

Service groups within the community will find micropublishing worthwhile to serve their own needs and to extend their reach. So will other community clubs and groups.

Once one or two of your patrons or community groups have micropublished books, they may be willing to do workshops for others who would be interested. With appropriate publicity and early examples of the resulting books, a significant percentage of your community may show interest. Every community is rich with people having special interests, distinctive personal knowledge, and local connections. It's possible that at least 10 percent of your patrons really do have books in them, ones that may not make commercial sense but that offer stories—history, knowledge, perspectives—that at least a few others will want to read. Micropublishing makes that feasible and inexpensive; your library can and should be a center for this creative activity.

The library is a natural center for creativity and for sharing. Where better to form editing circles, where thoughtful, literate people can improve one another's writing? With micropublishing tools, once the words are right, the rest is straightforward.

Library: Publisher or Facilitator?

Should your library be a micropublisher, or should it serve as a facilitator for micropublishers within the community?

The answer for many libraries will be yes—your library might very well serve both roles.

If you're publishing collections from writers' groups, youth groups, and other library groups, and those involved agree that profits should go to the library or the library's Friends group, it makes sense for the library to establish an imprint name and micropublish the books directly (or do so through your Friends or library foundation). That's also true if your library publishes local history and other works.

In most other cases, a more plausible library role is facilitator— offering advice (including copies of this book or photocopies of Chapters 4–6) and possibly tools, but not using the library's imprint or the library's Lulu or CreateSpace account. Your library probably doesn't want to extend its reputation to cover all books micropublished by community members—and you almost certainly don't want to set up an accounting operation to pass book profits through to the authors.

Is your Friends group a plausible home for some micropublishing? That depends on the group and your relationship with it. It's certainly worth discussing, as Friends could be a great source of assistance, and micropublishing could be a source of revenue.

Self-Publishing, Vanity Presses, and Micropublishing

If your library facilitates micropublishing, you're encouraging a special form of self-publishing. There's nothing wrong or shameful about self-publishing: It has a long and strong history and continues to be the source of some of the best books around (as well as many of the worst). Mark Twain was a self-publisher. It seems probable that technological and economic trends will make self-publishing more important and make the already vague boundaries among self-publishers, small publishers, and just plain *publishers* even fuzzier.

That's not new. There are tens of thousands of small publishers in the U.S. and around the world, and many of those small publishers started out as self-publishers. Micropublishing makes it easier but also allows micropublishers to avoid the overhead of small publishing.

Some commentators confuse self-publishing and micropublishing with vanity publishing. Vanity publishing is a very different economic model, although some contemporary firms have done a good job of making this boundary vague as well. Vanity publishers invite authors of books to submit manuscripts for review. A vanity press will typically applaud every manuscript submitted—and then let the author know about the "modest" costs to handle publication processes, costs that will run to thousands of dollars (or, with POD as the backend, possibly in the high hundreds of dollars).

Vanity publishers are imprints—but they're imprints that charge authors for editorial and production costs shouldered by regular publishers, making their profits up front rather than through book sales. In most cases, vanity publishers give lip service to editorial support and other publishing skills. In many cases, the author receives some number of bound books: The up-front costs may even be disguised as a minimum required order of books. In some cases, with actual books produced on demand, the author receives one copy and can purchase more. The book will be listed in *Books in Print*, and the publisher will probably register copyright.

That's where it stops. Unless the author pays even more, vanity publishers will not publicize the author's book in any meaningful way and are unlikely to succeed in distributing the book— especially since many vanity imprints are known by bookstores and libraries to have fairly crude publishing standards. Before beginning this project, I read a novel from my local library—by a local author, which probably overcame the imprint name. The text itself could have used a lot of editorial work but was no worse than some of what you'll see from trade publishers. But I noticed as I was reading that the book felt odd and realized why when I stepped back a bit from the sentences themselves.

Every paragraph in the book was indented. That's a minor point; some trade publishers leave things this way to save time. More to the point, although the text was justified, there was no hyphenation — which meant that many lines had enough space between words to interfere with reading.

As far as I could tell, the author's manuscript had been "typeset" by dumping it into a canned book template without further inspection. There were no widows (a single line stranded at the top of a page). "Orphan" in typography means both single lines stranded at the bottom of a page and short words or part of a word as the last line of a paragraph. The book had none of the former (stranded lines), but many of the latter (very short last lines of paragraphs). Note that Microsoft Word and other word processing programs control for widows and the first kind of orphan by default, but do nothing to prevent paragraphs from having very short last lines.

The author paid to have this work done. The author could have produced a more readable book herself and saved thousands of dollars by becoming a micropublisher, using the tools and advice in this book.

I believe there's a simple distinction between the service agencies that fulfill self-publishing and agencies that are, at least in part, vanity publishers. If an agency requires up-front fees for anything more than a single proof copy of a book, it is at least partly a vanity publisher. A proper fulfillment agency can and should offer lots of services for fees, but it should never require an author to use those services or pay for services the author neither needs nor wishes to use.

Walking the Talk: This Book and Micropublishing

I've micropublished several books since 2007, including a few that weren't expected to sell more than one or two copies (annual paperback versions of *Cites & Insights*, my free ejournal), one that has sold several hundred copies (*Balanced Libraries*), and several that have had very small sales. My wife has micropublished two volumes of family history for two branches of her family, and by the time this book appears, she may have produced new books based on handed-down stories from her extended family.

This book uses the tools of micropublishing, even though the trade paperback edition is traditionally published by Information Today, Inc. (ITI). It's traditionally published so it will reach as many libraries and community members as possible, and it has the editorial advantages of professional editing (and professional indexing)—but I prepared the layout and the template (with advice from the professionals at ITI). Apart from the cover, Microsoft Office 2010 on Windows 7 is the only software used to create this book. Specifically:

➢ I created the book template bk6pv.dotx (Book, 6" x 9", Palatino and Verdana) using Word 2010. That book template is available for downloading; see details in Chapter 4.

➢ I used Word 2010 for all writing, editing, and layout. I used Microsoft Excel 2010 to keep track of chapters during the writing and revision, but I could have done that with a table in Word.

➢ While ITI professionals provided line editing and copyediting suggestions as well as proofreading, I made all actual changes, and did copyfitting and page balancing in Word.

➢ The index was prepared by ITI, then sent to me as a Word document, which I imported into the book document.

➢ The PDF version was created using Office 2010's "Save as PDF" function, with the PDF/A option checked (see Chapter 9). (For efficiency reasons, a visually identical but smaller PDF was created using Adobe Acrobat 9.)

ITI prepared the cover. For previous micropublished books, I've generated covers using Paint.NET (or, in some cases, old versions of Corel PhotoPaint) to trim and modify existing photographs and overlay cover and spine type. For one book—used as an example in Chapter 10—I created the cover using nothing but Lulu's built-in tools.

A Few Key Terms

A few terms will be used frequently in portions of this book. They're also in the glossary.

Pica: One of two key measures of type size and spacing used throughout this book. In modern publishing, a pica is one-sixth of an inch—there are six picas to an inch. A 6" x 9" book (like this one) is also 36 picas wide and 54 picas tall. Most overall measurements and spacing measurements are in picas.

Point: The key measurement for type itself. There are 12 points to a pica or 72 points to an inch. Points are also used for smaller space measurements. For example, the body type for this book is 10 point Palatino Linotype set with 3 point leading (extra space between lines), sometimes stated as "10 on 13" or "10 over 13."

Microsoft Word and **Microsoft Office:** This book was prepared using Word 2010, but I generally refer to Word and Office rather than specific versions. As noted in Chapter 3, other than full PDF generation, earlier versions of Word should be able to do everything discussed in this book.

The Rest of This Book

I wrote this book for librarians and for authors. Librarians need to think about this chapter and Chapter 13 (particularly academic librarians). Every author should at least skim through Chapters 2–12. Most authors will want to spend extra time with Chapters 4 through 6 as they're working on their books, and ITI and I have agreed to allow Chapters 4 through 6 to be photocopied (on a limited basis) as an allowed use. (See the copyright page for details.)

While the rest of the book isn't divided into formal sections, there are four informal sections, as follows.

Chapters 1–3: Micropublishing Background

This chapter is just the beginning of a thorough background discussion of micropublishing.

Chapter 2 offers a quick introduction to the steps and processes involved in creating a book and shows how micropublishing affects each step. It's useful to consider how much extra effort (beyond writing) micropublishing may involve and where important processes may fall by the wayside if you don't pay attention.

Chapter 3 discusses this book's approach to micropublishing—a low-cost/no-cost approach using software you and your community members probably already own. Where additional software may be required, Chapter 3 includes low-cost options. Chapter 3 also discusses the two primary no-cost micropublishing service providers, Lulu and Create-Space—what they do, how they do it, and what they don't do.

Chapters 4–6: Layout and Typography— The Heart of Micropublishing

These chapters are aimed directly at authors and editors—those actually doing micropublishing. Chapter 4 discusses Word templates and the bk6pv.dotx and bk6pvex.dotx templates created to support this book and available for your use. I show why you should always use Word styles rather than tabs and spaces for headings and other formatting, and how to modify the existing template to change the look of your book.

Chapter 5 discusses layout decisions and includes examples of typefaces you might consider and other layout options. Chapter 5 looks a little different, as it is heavily composed of actual samples of options discussed—including some options you'll want to avoid and why.

Chapter 6 tells you specifically what you need to do to improve the look and readability of your book from so-so to top notch: a few techniques to get professional results without paying for new software or steep learning curves. You'll want to review this chapter once or twice as you finish writing and editing your book and get closer to actual publication.

Chapters 7–10: Special Topics in Micropublishing

Once you write a book-length manuscript and follow the steps in Chapters 4–6, you'll have the body of your book ready to go—but there's more to a book than just the body.

Chapter 7 discusses the stuff that comes before and after the body—front matter and back matter.

Chapter 8 considers choices for creating a cover for your book and what you need to know in order to do it entirely on your own. It also deals with extras and outsourcing: Whether you need an ISBN, what you should do about copyright, what you can pay to have done, and sample prices for outsourcing.

Chapter 9 is, for most authors, the final stage of publication: making sure your PDF is right and dealing with Lulu or CreateSpace.

Chapter 9 also discusses special cases for PDF, cases where you'll need or want more than the built-in PDF support in Office.

Chapter 10 deals with books other than perfect-bound paperbacks consisting of text, monochrome graphs, and line drawings. You can't include a few pages of glossy photographs in a regular micropublished book. You can't even include a multicolor graph. This chapter discusses special considerations for photographs and options for color. Depending on your supplier, you can also produce hardcover books and, in some cases, use special bindings; Chapter 10 discusses those options and also offers quick notes on ebooks.

Chapters 11–13: Now That Your Book Is Complete

You have your first copy. It looks great! You've made the book available for purchase by others (unless this is a truly private micropublished book). Now what?

Chapter 11 provides notes and resources for the most essential step if you hope for substantial sales: publicity and marketing. This chapter also considers options for a micropublication that turns out to be more successful than anticipated.

Chapter 12, primarily intended for academic librarians, considers the special case of journals published online and how you can serve the typically small number of authors, readers, and librarians who want proper print copies, especially shelf copies of each full volume.

Chapter 13 offers a few concluding notes, including comments on why publishers still matter.

Finally, a glossary provides definitions for key terms used in the book, and a brief bibliography notes sources consulted while writing this book and additional sources that you may find useful.

First Have Something to Say

The primary title for my first professionally published book of the 21st century is *First Have Something to Say: Writing for the Library Profession*, published by ALA Editions in 2003.

It's also the key piece of advice for any would-be micropublisher. *First have something to say:* an idea that you can turn into a worthwhile book. That book may be you working alone; it may be a collection from a group.

I can't help you write your book. There are many places to go for advice on how to write and how to improve your writing; there's even a little advice in the book I just cited.

Before you start putting your words into chapters on your computer, read Chapter 4 or at least take this piece of early advice: Use Word's styles for your headings and other aspects of layout—don't simulate styles by changing the typeface, size, alignment, and spacing manually. Using styles will save you time down the road, as you won't have to undo manual changes in order to ensure a consistent overall look.

Once you're sure you have something worth publishing, use the rest of this book to help you make the best book you possibly can. You don't need to spend money to do that; you do need to spend time and pay attention. The results are worth it.

You have something to say. Micropublishing can help you say it as effectively and economically as possible.

2
Publishing and Micropublishing

Publishing a book involves many processes. Some can be skipped, some can be combined, but all play some role in moving from an author's idea to a successful book. Before looking at micropublishing and what's covered in the rest of this book, consider the steps in book publishing in general.

Throughout this chapter, "you" may refer either to the author or to the library. I'll try to make it clear when the library is or can be directly involved.

Steps in Book Publishing

It begins with an idea—usually an author's idea, although an editor or publisher may have the initial idea. It ends, ideally, with a book that reaches its target audience and yields appropriate rewards—financial and otherwise—for its author.

Between those steps is the publishing process. I've seen it described several ways, generally involving the processes noted here and sometimes additional steps. The steps may not always be in this order and some steps may overlap, but a book typically involves these steps:

Idea and writing: First comes the manuscript—beginning with an idea, continuing through research and rough draft, and ending with something that feels like a book.

Rewriting and initial editing: Few first drafts are ready to print and publish as they stand. A good writer may spend more time rewriting than writing the first draft and may seek the help of others in reviewing and editing the manuscript.

Acquisition/acceptance: An acquisition editor may have approved a contract for a book based only on the idea, but at some point the editor must determine that the manuscript is acceptable before it enters the publisher's portion of the process.

Line editing: Line editors—sometimes called editors—work with the manuscript and the author to improve the manuscript, suggesting or requiring revisions as small as changing a word and as large as cutting, adding, or moving whole sections. Some line editors completely rework manuscripts, moving whole sections and slashing through text; others offer light revisions.

Copyediting: Where line editing, sometimes just called editing, may lead to major revisions and rewrites, copyediting is all about details: Checking for grammar and punctuation but also assuring consistency in spelling, capitalization, hyphenation, and stylistic issues. For fiction (and some nonfiction), a copyeditor ensures that names are used consistently. Copyeditors also question factual issues and should be sensitive to issues of libel or copyright. Good copyediting ensures consistency throughout a book and should help assure good written style. That involves attention to detail and an awareness of stylistic elements—but also involves sensitivity to the style used by a writer, since copyediting should improve prose, not replace the writer's style with the copyeditor's style. (I'm combining two senses of "style" here: the style of writing and "house style," the rules for those elements that can be handled more than one way. Whether the name of a certain paper is the *New York Times* or *The New York Times* is a matter of house style; a preference for short sentences and paragraphs is part of writing style. In general, a line editor should offer more suggestions on writing style, whereas a copyeditor should ensure that the "house" style for a manuscript is consistent throughout.)

Authorial revisions: The author should have the final say in those editing decisions where more than one legitimate choice is possible. Once an author completes revisions, the book is ready for production steps. (Note that authorial revisions and some copyediting may follow layout and typography.)

Layout and typography: Decisions on layout and typography— typefaces, margins, size and placement of headings, etc.—may take place early on and will eventually lead to a set of page proofs in some form, with final page numbers and the like.

Proofreading: The purpose of proofreading is *only* to catch typographical errors and spelling errors, not to refine the copy.

Indexing: If a book has an index—most nonfiction books do, most fiction books do not—the index can't be prepared until layout, proofreading, and typography are complete.

Cover design: At some point prior to actual printing, somebody needs to design a cover for the book.

Printing and binding: The set of pages and the cover become a physical book.

Distribution, sales, and fulfillment: Copies of the book reach readers and libraries—through bookstores, online booksellers, websites, approval plans, or other means. In the process, orders must be taken, money must be collected, and books must be shipped.

Marketing and publicity: Through a combination of distributing press releases, sending copies to reviewers, advertising, and other means, publishers (and, typically, authors) make the book known to its potential readers.

What's Different in Micropublishing

Micropublishing—that is, preparing a book with standard desktop software and using Lulu (www.lulu.com) or CreateSpace (www.createspace.com) for the final product—eliminates some processes and modifies others.

Fundamentally Unchanged

Idea and writing: You still need an idea and need to turn that idea into a manuscript.

Rewriting and initial editing: If anything, these steps may be more important in micropublishing.

Authorial revisions: No matter who does the editing—even if only the author—at some point the author must decide that a manuscript is in its final state.

Cover design: This still needs to be done—but it's up to you to prepare a cover, hire someone to design one for you, or use your service provider's tools to prepare one.

Eliminated

Acquisition/acceptance: For most micropublishing, the author *is* in effect the publisher; there's no acceptance process.

That's the only step in book publishing that *inherently* disappears in micropublishing.

Still Required Through Other Means

Almost every book still benefits from line editing and copyediting. Every book needs layout and typography. Most nonfiction books need indexes. Proofreading is essential for *every* book.

Similarly, it's not a print book unless it's printed and bound; it's useless unless it's distributed in some form and orders are fulfilled; and without publicity of some form, the book might as well not exist.

Traditional publishers provide all of those services. Having to complete line editing, copyediting, layout, typography, indexing, and proofreading explains why a publisher may need half a year to two years or more to produce a book from an accepted manuscript. Printing and binding, distribution, and publicity turn the final manuscript into something tangible and continue until the book goes out of print.

Since there's no publisher to handle these steps, you need to handle them through other means.

What's Covered Here

The heart of this book is layout and typography.

That includes basic decisions such as the page size and margins and more interesting decisions such as choice of body typeface and type size, choice of heading or display typeface and size, how headings are handled, and the nature of running page headers and footers. Most of these decisions are embodied in a template. Chapter 4 discusses templates and how to modify them to suit your own tastes. Chapter 5 shows a range of type choices and typographic options and considers the decisions necessary to make a template work for you.

A good template used consistently will yield an acceptable book. But you can do much better without spending more on software. That's where Chapter 6 comes in: copyfitting and other ways to make your book as attractive, readable, and professional-looking as possible. Adhering to the advice in Chapter 6 involves extra work, but it can lead to a book that looks as good as most professional publications.

The rest of the book discusses other steps in the publishing process in less detail, except for the step-by-step process of dealing with a provider, covered in Chapter 10. I can't offer you a course in line editing or copyediting, and I'm wholly unqualified to tell you how to build a good index (although I can offer a few notes and warnings on using built-in indexing tools). Nor can I tell you how to market and publicize your book, although it should be clear that nobody else is going to do it for you—unless you pay.

What's Handled by Service Providers

The key to low-cost/no-cost micropublishing is a *service provider* with no up-front charges. The provider is not a publisher (or, in some cases, is a nominal publisher of record). Instead, the provider is a service agency, offering a set of publishing services based on producing individual books only when they're ordered, otherwise known as POD, print on demand.

I like to think of micropublishing as publish on demand, also abbreviated POD, to distinguish this use of one-at-a-time book production from the back-office POD that's now used by many publishers to keep books "in print" when it's no longer economical to print one copy or two thousand copies at a time. That standard use of POD also covers the growing number of in-house book production units such as the Espresso Book Machine, which could be used to support micropublishing but currently mostly produces public domain books or those published traditionally or as ebooks.

As of this writing, there are two service providers that fit the low-cost/no-cost model: Lulu and CreateSpace, a division of Amazon. Because Lulu offers a more flexible set of choices for book size, design, and binding, including hardcover books, and because Lulu is a little clearer about being a service provider, I use Lulu as the primary example in most chapters. But I've micropublished through both services (the same book in each case), and both will work.

Lulu and CreateSpace print and bind books, but only as they're ordered (by you or by customers). Both services handle distribution, sales, and fulfillment as needed: Customers order directly from them or indirectly through affiliated sites, and these services ship books directly to the customers, keeping part of the revenue for services rendered.

That's the pure micropublishing model, but you can also use Lulu and CreateSpace to produce small quantities of books that you'll sell yourself or through local bookstores. Lulu and CreateSpace *will* handle all fulfillment, but both companies will also be happy to ship you quantities of books to sell elsewhere.

Other Service Providers: Proceed With Caution

There are other companies that, at first glance, appear comparable to Lulu and CreateSpace—or maybe even better. From what I've seen, and assuming what you want to produce is a primarily textual paperback or hardcover (as opposed to a glossy photo collection or coffeetable book), I'd approach other companies with caution.

A straightforward service provider should meet all these tests:

➢ It should be clear that the author retains copyright.

➢ The author should be able to take a book to another provider or publisher at any time with no conditions other than removing a provider's ISBN.

➢ The author should never be required to purchase more than one book at a time, and there should be no required costs other than one proof copy of the book.

➢ The author should set the retail price of a book (as long as it's more than the stated production costs).

➢ The provider should clearly state how and how often net proceeds (either stated as royalties or as net proceeds) are paid to the author.

➢ The provider's online bookstore should work and have some evidence of activity.

➢ The provider should typically *not* call itself a publisher.

➢ The provider's website should focus on what it does for authors, not on why you should *not* use other services.

If any of those conditions isn't met, be suspicious. Do some searching on Bing or Google. See what other users have to say about the company. If possible, check the Better Business Bureau rating of the company. Check Writer Beware (www.sfwa.org/for-authors/writer-beware). Chances are, what looks like a straightforward service provider is actually some variety of vanity publisher, although that might not always be the case.

Dealing With Other Steps

What about those other steps? In some cases, groups in your library may be able to help—and the library might even establish a clearinghouse to help or work with you and others to establish a micropublishers' group. In other cases, you may be on your own.

You should have others look at your manuscript even before you're sure you want to turn it into a book. Does your library have a writers' group? If you're writing a family history, is there a genealogical group with members who might be willing to help? Your friends and family may also be excellent sources—if you can convince them to offer honest advice, not just shine you on. (If your book consists entirely of oral histories and written reminiscences from others, you don't need much editorial review—but you still need proofreading.)

What works for initial revisions may also work for line editing and copyediting. Can you do both yourself as the author? Yes, you can—but you need to have someone else edit your work at least once. You can become too close to your work to step back and see things clearly. An outsider will catch errors and ambiguities you're likely to overlook. Are there others within your social or library circles who might be willing to do this? Is it worth paying for?

Think about the difference between line editing and copyediting. Micropublishing may combine the two roles into a single pass, but that involves two very different ways of looking at a manuscript. A line editor looks at the book as a whole and how paragraphs and chapters flow within that whole. A copyeditor focuses primarily on sentences and consistency.

Proofreading requires yet a third way of examining a manuscript. Fortunately, Word itself provides a first level of defense, with a good spell-checker and an occasionally useful (albeit frequently wrong) grammar checker. Unfortunately, *that's not enough*: No spell-checker can catch cases where you've chosen an existing word that isn't the word you intended, and mechanical grammar checkers can only go so far. Most likely, proofreading and copyediting will overlap, in which case your final revisions need to be done carefully so you don't introduce new errors. At least word processing minimizes actual mechanical errors—Word almost never repeats a word on its own or omits a line of type accidentally.

There are people who love to index and have spent years honing their indexing skills. If you can find someone who fits this category, you're in luck—indexing can be one of the most difficult and thankless tasks in publishing. If there's a step other than cover design that may be worth paying for, it's this one: A good index makes a nonfiction book far more useful. Chapter 7 considers some aspects of indexing and other front and back matter in a book.

You may not need marketing and publicity for some micropublishing. If you're publishing a family history strictly for your own immediate family, all you need to do is let them know about it or send them copies. But if you hope to reach a wider audience, you need a marketing and publicity plan. Chapter 12 offers some notes, but certainly not anything comprehensive.

Micropublishing Works—
But It's Not Magic

You can use this book and the software you probably own to create a book that looks as good as most trade paperbacks, especially trade paperbacks now being produced using POD tools. (Some people will notice the difference in quality between offset lithography, used for most traditional books, and laser printing, used for most POD books—but as books go into the backlist, that difference disappears.)

You can get that book into print with no cost other than the price of your own copy. The rest of this book will help you achieve high layout quality and improve the chances that your "proof copy" will be the last copy you *need* to buy.

More to the point, for libraries working with community members and for most of us who don't have the capital or the desire to become real publishers, *this stuff works*. Lulu creates trade paperbacks and hardcover books that are equal in quality to backlist books from any standard publisher, with better paper than that offered in many trade books. CreateSpace does the same for paperbacks, although it doesn't offer hardcover books. In most cases, CreateSpace will get your book into Amazon automatically—and in many cases, so will Lulu.

But neither one is magic. Neither will create a great cover for free. Neither will turn your manuscript into a polished set of pages for free. Neither will automatically get your books into bookstores (if that's what you want), send out review copies, advertise your book, or otherwise publicize it—at least not without charging a hefty price. That's all up to you. I've done a micropublished book (*Balanced Libraries*) that's yielded as much revenue as some traditionally published books I've written; I've also done one that sold a total of three copies.

If you're micropublishing to suit a specialized need, fewer than a dozen copies may be precisely what you need—in which case micropublishing is a great solution. But micropublishing won't turn you into a best-selling author, and very few micropublished books achieve bestseller status. If your book does turn out to be a surprise success? Read Chapter 12. One great thing about Lulu and CreateSpace is that you're free to take your book elsewhere.

Don't Expect Perfection

Good publishers have access to many more first-rate typefaces than you probably do. Good book designers will use those typefaces intelligently based on the nature of a book and are likely to achieve more polished and interesting layout and typography than you will just using and modifying templates. Good editing is important to a book's worth.

On the other hand, many (probably most) mainstream books don't receive high-quality individual layout attention. Most of those I've sampled seem to use a few basic templates and ignore the fine points of polished typography. You may not have the range of typeface options that big publishers do, but you can provide the attention to detail that seems to be missing from books published by some of the biggest publishers.

If a book has anticipated sales of fewer than 100 copies, it's a moot point: You can't justify spending the money for professional layout, typography, and printing. The templates and advice in this book will get you most of the way there. You'll be able to produce a book that's well designed and more readable in some ways than most big-publisher books, even without the wealth of typeface options and quality of offset or letterpress printing.

Resources

Copyediting: A Practical Guide by Karen Judd may offer far more detail than you need but also offers useful advice. My library has the original 1982 edition (Los Altos: William Kaufmann, 1982), portions of which are badly dated; a 2001 edition is now available.

How to Get Happily Published by Judith Appelbaum (New York: Harper-Perennial, 1992) offers a broad, useful commentary on traditional publishing and self-publishing. Much of the advice is also pertinent to micropublishing, specifically comments and resources for writing, editing, and—perhaps most important—publicity and marketing.

3
The Low-Cost/No-Cost Approach

Any good book requires a fair amount of effort. Every traditionally published book also requires a fair amount of money, and that's been true for self-published books as well.

That doesn't have to be the case. If you have an ordinary computer with the most commonly used software and access to broadband, you don't need to spend a dime to micropublish a book until you order the first (or proof) copy—and that includes spending money on new software. That's one reason micropublishing is so attractive as a public library service: It doesn't require new funding to add this new service, either on the library's or (in most cases) on the writer's part.

You've written a book or are planning to write a book using a current version of Microsoft Word on Windows or a Mac? *You're all set* for micropublishing; you can skip to the section "Low-Cost Assumptions" later in this chapter. If you want a quick once-over as to just how much traditional publishing costs, read on. If you're not willing to pay for Word, move to "No-Cost Alternatives" near the end of this chapter.

Why Publishing Is Expensive

If you've already read Chapter 2, you have some idea why traditional publishing is expensive—why most books require close to $10,000 (and quite possibly several times that much) to move from manuscript to bound book. It's not about editors lighting Cuban cigars with $100 bills and taking authors to three-martini lunches at Four Seasons; it's about real costs for real processes.

Since I've never been part of the publishing industry, I won't attempt to estimate numbers for each step, although there are some sample costs later in this chapter. Think about a 200-page trade paperback (50,000 to 60,000 words)—a short novel or a medium-length nonfiction book. Think about how long you'd expect an acquisitions editor to spend dealing with the author and shepherding the project, how long you'd expect a line editor to take doing a thorough editing job, the time a good copyeditor will need to make sure everything's right. Now pay for the interior designer to design the layout and typography—and somebody to turn that design into actual pages (which may be a text artisan working with advanced desktop publishing software, noting that the text artisan may be the designer or copyeditor). Add the costs of proofreading. Good indexing doesn't come cheap, and neither do professional cover design and illustration.

As I jot down plausible numbers for each of these steps and assume modest but not minimum wages for most of the well-educated, highly skilled people doing them, I find it hard not to hit $10,000 before printing and binding. Add another $3,000 to print and bind the first 1,000 copies, and you're up to $13,000—before promotion, review copies, distribution, and all that.

People who work in publishing are probably laughing at these numbers as being absurdly low (except for printing costs, where the numbers should be fairly solid). On the other hand, some vanity publishers and packagers can charge considerably less, because they're shortchanging some or all of the processes.

Why Self-Publishing Is Expensive

Self-publishing eliminates the acquisitions editor and corporate overhead. Those are the only costs that go away. A self-publisher using traditional techniques must add the cost of storage for the supply of printed books (which may be a garage) and, for some self-publishers who formerly had self-employment income, the cost and complexity of changing from cash accounting to accrual accounting for IRS purposes.

Consider some other costs, using Lulu and CreateSpace charges for additional services you can outsource to them and examples of proposed charges found on the web. Where stated, I've used the price for 50,000- to 60,000-word manuscripts. Lulu and CreateSpace offer packages of services, as do vanity publishers who require up-front fees to publish your book under their imprints. Packages at CreateSpace that include some level of marketing run from $2,500 to $5,000; packages at Lulu are divided into pre-publishing ($630 to $4,700), marketing ($2,900 to $9,500), and distribution options such as offering your books to Ingram and Amazon ($25 to $75); figure $3,500 to $14,000 total.

Line Editing

CreateSpace offers editorial evaluation at $299 for fewer than 60,000 words ($399 for 60,000 to 100,000 words)—but the evaluation doesn't claim to be a replacement for good line editing. Lulu offers editorial quality review for $199—but that uses a "professional copy editor" who recommends the level of editing your manuscript *really* needs. This is not the full charge. Sampling advertised editing services using 60,000 words as a target, I see prices from $800 to $2,700.

Copyediting

CreateSpace offers what it calls comprehensive copyediting—apparently a combination of line editing and copyediting. For a 60,000-word manuscript, the price would be $1,140. Basic copyediting, omitting line editing, would cost $1,050, and what CreateSpace calls comprehensive copy-editing plus, "specifically for first-time authors and writers who speak English as a second language," would cost $1,920.

Lulu doesn't state prices for copyediting; you get quotes after the $199 editorial review. A "mechanical edit" for a very short manuscript—7,500 words or fewer—is $150, which might suggest a price of about $1,200 for line editing and copyediting of a 60,000-word manuscript.

Most editing services seem to combine line editing and copyedit-ing. In one case, what I'd think of as copyediting would be $1,140 for 60,000 words.

Layout and Typography

There are so many levels of design assistance that it's hard to judge prices—and the cost of actual typography depends heavily on whether a self-publisher plans to generate her own PDF or use professional typesetting.

CreateSpace charges $299 for a service that provides a set of options for interior design and turns a manuscript into a PDF based on the author's choice of those options—or $499 for a custom design. Lulu charges $249 for basic text formatting (with no images), with the choice of six interior layout and corrections for some typical formatting problems—or $699 for "ultimate formatting," which also offers six interior layouts but also a choice of body and heading typefaces. One self-publishing service agency charges $250 to $350 for standard fiction and prose nonfiction layout.

Full typesetting? Given a Word manuscript, I see prices as low as $4 per page ($800 for a 200-page book), but also $6 ($1,200 for 200 pages) and higher. In all cases, "typesetting" means importing the Word manuscript into a higher-end layout program such as QuarkXPress or Adobe InDesign, and preparing a PDF.

Proofreading

Proofreading charges tend to be bundled with copyediting charges, although ideally proofreading takes place *after* copyediting and layout are done. Let's assume for now that good copyediting will cover proofreading.

Indexing

Neither CreateSpace nor Lulu offers indexing as a priced service—and you can bet neither one will do it for free! Elsewhere, I've seen quotes as low as $2 per page and as high as $6 per page, with one major service supplier charging $3.75 per page for 6" x 9" books. Most prices seem to be in the $3 to $5 range. Figuring that a 200-page book probably has about 190 indexable pages, an index is likely to cost $570 to $950—and a really good index may cost $1,000 or more.

Cover Design

Unless you choose to upload your own cover, CreateSpace charges $299 for its simplest cover option, in which you choose from a range of existing formats, background colors, and typefaces, and add your own uploaded image. If you want something more distinctive, CreateSpace charges $499 or $999 (depending on how much design time you want), or $1,499 if you want a custom illustration.

Similarly, Lulu has three levels in addition to the Cover Wizard: $115 for a template-based design, $450 for an original design, and $999 for a premium design (three design choices), although even the most expensive option doesn't include custom illustrations.

Other prices seem similar—one service agency offers four levels from $149 to $1,195 and another charges $250 to $600. Most medium-priced options include some choice of stock photos.

Printing and Binding

For CreateSpace and Lulu, printing and binding are part of fulfill-ment and based on a binding charge for each copy and a charge per page, although both offer discounts for quantity purchases. Both are expensive on a per-copy basis compared to other book printers, largely because books are produced one at a time and the charge includes fulfillment. For example, Lulu charges $8.50 per copy plus shipping for a 200-page paperback, while CreateSpace charges $5.50 per copy plus shipping for a 200-page paperback.

For traditional printers, producing 6" x 9" paperbacks, the price will depend heavily on quantity. So, for example, one printer that quotes in 16-page signatures wants $895 to print and bind 50 copies of a 192-page paperback, $3,150 for 500 copies, or $5,660 for 1,000 copies. Another, limiting options to 5.5" x 8.5" or 8.5" x 11", charges $496 for 100 copies of a 200-page book, $1,440 for 500 copies, or $2,400 for 1,000 copies. Yet another charges $362 for 50 copies, $2,250 for 500 copies, or $3,460 for 1,000 copies. (I haven't used these sup-pliers and can't comment on production quality.) The price per copy can be considerably lower than for Lulu or CreateSpace, but only when you're buying a substantial number of copies.

Distribution, Sales, and Fulfillment

What will it cost you to get books into bookstores and fulfill direct orders? For the latter, you probably need to obtain a credit card mer-chant's account and the software that goes with it. Factor in packages and actual postage for fulfillment. It's not cheap to sell books yourself, unless you sell them when you're speaking at seminars and other events (as quite a few self-publishers do).

Marketing

When it comes to marketing, the sky's the limit. One book on self-publishing notes that a book publicist will charge $2,000 to $4,000 a month as a retainer—and you'll need one for several months. Sending out review copies isn't that expensive—the cost of the books plus, say, $4 to $5 for each recipient for packing and shipping—but you need to know *who* to send review copies to, and if you plan for wide coverage, you're still talking hundreds of dollars.

CreateSpace is only too happy to sell marketing support, and those prices may indicate just how expensive marketing can be. A press release with distribution runs $598 ($199 *without* distribution). You'll pay $495 to get a Kirkus Indie review you can use on Amazon, on your cover, and elsewhere—or $595 if you want it in five weeks rather than ten; add $399 or $549 for a *ForeWord* Clarion review. Add $799 for "social networking account creation," $499 for a publicity kit, and on, and on … including, for those enamored of video book trailers, $1,249 for a 30-second trailer or $2,299 for a 60-second trailer with narration. You see a similarly wide range of prices at Lulu, including three marketing packages running $2,900 to $9,500. Individual services include items such as $650 for a press release, $950 for a targeted media list, $199 to $575 for various reviews, and $300 to $600 for website design.

Putting It All Together

Self-publishing through traditional means is not practical unless you believe you can sell at least 500 copies. Consider the set of costs here. I don't see how you could get by for much less than $8,000 to have 500 copies of a 200-page book edited, designed, printed, and marketed—and only about $1,800 of that represents the difference between 50 copies and 500 copies. That's $16 a copy, but it's also $8,000 out of pocket.

I've seen package prices that appear to be much lower from some of the author-pays "publishers." But based on examples I've seen, I don't think you're getting your money's worth.

Back-End Savings From Micropublishing

If you want to publish your family history and know it will only appeal to a handful of family members, none of the numbers just discussed makes sense. You're not willing to spend $6,000 to get ten copies of a 200-page paperback; you're probably not willing to spend $1,000 or even $399.

You don't need marketing—you know your market. You'll find ways to do some editing, copyediting, and proofreading. You don't need a fancy cover.

Lulu and CreateSpace may be happy to sell you all those services, but in my experience they don't pressure you to buy them—and without optional services, there's no advance cost at all. More to the point, both Lulu and CreateSpace are designed for niche books: They're most cost-effective when you're selling one book at a time. A price of $5.50 or $8.50 may sound high for a 200-page book, but that's the price for *one book*, not the per-book price on a 500-copy order. If you're selling books to other people, that price (plus a percentage of the actual price you set) includes fulfillment: a webpage describing the book, an order mechanism, credit card handling, and shipping.

That's why this book assumes you'll use one of these services. They are not the most cost-effective ways to become a self-publisher with a 1,000-copy initial run. They are the only cost-effective ways to produce five copies of a book for your family or 50 copies of a book for a niche market.

Low-Cost Assumptions

The heart of this book is options and instructions for effective layout and typography: how to make your micropublication look as good as most professionally published books. I'm assuming you'll use friends and acquaintances to substitute for some of the fee-based activities. That leaves software.

If you have a recent version of Word—2010 for Windows, 2008 or newer for the Macintosh—and Windows 7 or Macintosh OS X, you're set: That's all the software you need. It's the software I used for the interior of this book: Word 2010 running on Windows 7. You're *much* better off if you've moved up from Microsoft Office 2007 or Word 2007: You have a much stronger collection of typefaces.

If you have an older version of Word, you may need PDF generation software or a PDF printer driver. The key requirement here is that you must be able to embed *all* typefaces in your PDF, including a hidden use of Arial that seems to pop up everywhere in Word—and regular PDF options don't embed Arial. If there's an option for PDF/A, that's what you need: This archival version necessarily embeds everything. If you need to buy PDF software, you should be able to find packages for $30 to $70, and you may find free downloadable software. That said, Adobe Acrobat—likely to cost between $110 and $250—will do a better job of producing compact PDFs. (For example, the book used in Chapter 9 to illustrate the uploading process is a 4.9 megabyte PDF as produced directly from Word—or a 1.05 megabyte PDF as produced by Adobe Acrobat with all typefaces embedded.)

If you want to design your own cover rather than using the cover wizard at your service provider, you may need graphics software to prepare a design, touch up photos, and add type to the cover and spine. A package such as Corel Paint Shop Pro at around $50 or Adobe Photoshop Elements at around $80 may be the most user-friendly inexpensive way to get more than enough power for creating book covers—but I've found Paint.NET (www.getpaint.net), a free download, quite acceptable if a little more cumbersome. If you don't mind the learning curve, the GIMP (www.gimp.org), another free download, provides plenty of power. Paint.NET is a Windows program. There are versions of the GIMP for UNIX but also for Windows and Mac OS X.

Partial screen shots in this book did not require use of additional software. If you have Windows 7, you should be aware of the Snipping Tool—key "snip" in the program search menu to find it, at which point you may want to add a shortcut on the desktop. Snipping Tool lets you select any rectangle on your screen (or, for that matter, do a free-form selection), annotate and touch up the selection, and save it in PNG, GIF, JPEG, or HTML form with a filename and location you determine.

Why Not Use High-End Layout Software?

Most books these days are probably laid out using QuarkXPress or Adobe InDesign. Designers may claim, with some justification, that those programs will do a better job on your book than Word. If you plan to do a series of books and want the best possible layout and typography, you might want to consider one of these programs. I haven't mentioned them in this book because, for both the library and its patrons, they violate not only the low-cost/no-cost guideline but also the effort to make this a straightforward process.

You probably know how to use Word, or at least its primary functions. The chapters that follow will show you what you need to know to make Word function well for book production. You probably *don't* know how to use QuarkXPress or InDesign; both of them have fairly steep learning curves. And they don't come free. QuarkXPress sells for $800 or so. InDesign goes for $600 or more. Add to that tens of hours to understand the programs and get them to work the way you want. It's all reasonable if you design books for a living; it's absurd if you're doing a book or two.

I have never used QuarkXPress or InDesign. I did use Ventura Publisher to lay out and typeset several books (including *Future Libraries: Dreams, Madness & Reality* and *Being Analog: Creating Tomorrow's Libraries*, both from ALA Editions, the first coauthored with Michael Gorman). I stopped using it because, when it was moved from the early GEM visual environment to Windows and changed ownership, it became unstable. Are the books I did with Ventura better in layout and more polished than the books you can do with Word, using the techniques in this book? Not appreciably so—and maybe not at all.

No-Cost Alternatives

You say you don't have Word, or, for that matter, Windows or Mac OS X? You're not out of luck: It's possible to do micropublishing with *no* software costs (assuming you have a computer), although it will be more cumbersome and you may not achieve results that are quite as good.

You'll need LibreOffice (www.libreoffice.org) or OpenOffice (www.openoffice.org), at this point essentially identical open source office suites. I'll refer to LibreOffice throughout this book, as it's not affiliated with a major corporation. Both suites include PDF output with PDF/A options, so that part's covered. Both suites are available to download for Windows, Macintosh, and Linux, and both are free.

In addition to the downloadable Word templates provided in conjunction with this book—one with sample text and sample front matter sections, the other a pure template—I've provided a downloadable LibreOffice/OpenOffice template, but it's not as complete or useful as the Word templates.

Where feasible, I've provided notes in Chapters 4–6 on using LibreOffice to lay out your book, but without illustrations and with somewhat less experience. The way LibreOffice handles templates presents some difficulties. It's not clear to me that LibreOffice can handle chapters and complex running headers and footers as well as Word does, and copyfitting by condensing paragraphs is much more cumbersome because LibreOffice's methodology requires many more keystrokes. I don't believe LibreOffice supports vertical justification at all.

This is not to say that you shouldn't or can't use LibreOffice to prepare a good-looking micropublication. It's a remarkably sound office suite for the price, and the Write program does include support for tables of contents, indexes, hyphenation, kerning, and most of what you need to do the job. You may find it more than satisfactory—and if you hate the ribbon in Word 2007 and beyond, you'll love the traditional menu look of LibreOffice.

When Cheap Can Turn Expensive

Micropublishing makes enormous sense for some books, but it's not the best way to go in all cases.

If your book has substantial sales potential or if you're uneasy about your own writing (and unable to locate good, honest editors you can deal with), various levels of professional editing may be bargains for what they accomplish. The same goes for proofreading and indexing. And you may not be able to reach that sales potential without good marketing.

I would have said that micropublishing on the cheap is also expensive when you *achieve* large sales levels—when bookstores want hundreds of copies of your book. That may not be as true as it used to be, as micropublishing service agencies offer large-quantity printing that may be competitive.

Micropublishing doesn't work very well in these cases:

➤ You need high-quality photographs in a book that's primarily text, or you want a few color pages in a long book. You can print full color or photographic quality, but you'll pay several times as much for each book, as the per-page price jumps from 2 cents (or so) to 15 or 20 cents (or more!).

➤ You need to sell books through a range of bookstores around the world, and you need to let those bookstores know about the book. At that point, you're looking at traditional self-publishing.

➤ You're assuming that many libraries will buy your book. That's a difficult assumption for self-publishing of any nature.

➢ You're cavalier about using large excerpts from other books or photos that you didn't take, or you're ready to say strong, negative things about people but can't necessarily prove those things. You can get yourself into serious and very expensive legal trouble when you infringe copyright or commit libel—and traditional publishers may help prevent this sort of problem.

However, for most niche books that you and other community members are likely to create, low-cost/no-cost micropublishing will serve your needs.

4
Dealing With Templates

The first step in preparing a professional-looking book with Microsoft Word is to use styles and a good book template, one you can make your own. There haven't been any good general-purpose book templates for Word (at least not that I've been able to find)—so, with help from Information Today, Inc.'s (ITI) designers, I created a fairly simple one that you can download, customize, and use.

We'll get to that template and how you can modify it after a few notes about styles and why you should make a habit of using them. Read this chapter *before* you write your book, if possible: It will save you time down the road.[1]

Why Use Styles?

If you're like many other Word users, you don't think about styles at all. When you have a heading or subheading, you change the typeface and size and make other formatting changes directly in the text. Why change now?

The main reasons to use styles are that you can assure consistent usage throughout your book, and you can think about the specific layout of your book after you've written it, without having to undo or redo a lot of work. There's another excellent reason: If you use

---

[1] Chapters 4–6 of this book may be photocopied by libraries and schools for limited non-commercial distribution to patrons and students. See "Permission to Photocopy" on the copyright page for terms and conditions.

the right styles, your table of contents requires no effort to generate or maintain.

If you're using Word, you *are* using styles and a template. Specifically, you're using the Normal style and the Normal template. There's no way to avoid using styles and templates, so you should take advantage of them.

If you've never thought about styles and templates, try this experiment. (Note that here, and for the rest of the book, I use sans serif text to indicate options you see or type in Word or on a service provider's website.) Open a Word 2010 or Word 2007 document you've written or downloaded—any document will do. With the cursor in any paragraph and the Home tab's ribbon visible, look at the right-hand Styles section of the ribbon: Normal should be outlined in yellow. Point to Normal and right-click. Select Modify from the right-click menu. You'll get a dialog box with a Format pull-down at the bottom and a lot of information about the Normal style, as well as some of the formatting options that also appear in the Font and Paragraph sections of the ribbon. Go to the Formatting section and select Chiller from the typeface menu, 16 from the size menu, and the centered-text button. Check out what's happened to your text—not just the current paragraph, but *all* of it. (If you don't see changes, click OK. After you've looked at it, the Undo button will reverse the changes.)

Pretty dramatic, isn't it? Because all your paragraphs are in the Normal style, modifying that style modifies every paragraph. Now, if your chapter names were all in Heading 1 style, headings within chapters were all in Heading 2, and subheadings were in Heading 3, you could make similarly consistent changes—just by modifying the style.

Unlearning Direct Formatting Habits

Do you hit a tab at the start of each new paragraph to provide an indentation? *Stop.* Modify the Normal style (right-click on Normal, choose Modify), choosing Paragraph on the Format pull-down. On the Indents and Spacing tab in the Indentation section, change Special to First line with 1 pi as a value. That will automatically indent each new paragraph one pica (one-sixth of an inch). If there's space above or space below the paragraph, you should change both of those values to 0: You normally need either indentation or space above a new paragraph, but not both.

If you have a long heading and you want to specify where a line break should come, do you hit Enter at that point? *Stop.* That doesn't start a new line; it starts a new paragraph, and once you use styles, that makes a big difference. Instead, insert a forced line break—the easiest way is to press Shift and Enter at the same time.

Did you change the typeface, size, and alignment of that heading, which was originally just text? *Stop.* Use a heading style instead.

The more you use styles for your formatting, the easier it is to assure consistency and make simple changes that modify your entire document without searching through each page.

Style Basics

If you're on the **Home** tab, six styles will appear in the **Styles** section. But if you click on the expansion mark (the little down-right arrow at the right edge of the **Styles** section), a styles palette will take over the right edge of your screen and be available no matter what tab you're on.

When you type a chapter title, click on **Heading 1** while you're in the heading. When you type a heading within a chapter, click on **Heading 2.** When you type a subheading, click on **Heading 3.**

When you change Normal paragraphs to headings, you will see the typography change. Don't worry about whether the resulting look is what you really want at this point. How it looks now isn't important. When you modify Heading 1 or another heading style, or copy your text into a new document using a new template, all Heading 1 cases will reflect the changes—automatically, without any effort on your part.

That may be all you need to know while you're writing the book. I'd do one more thing immediately, because it will save you some time when you're working on layout and typography: Add a **First** style.

Adding a First Style

Click on the leftmost icon at the bottom of the **Styles** palette, which shows **New style** as a tooltip if you hover the mouse over it. That opens up the **Create New Style** dialog box as shown in Figure 4.1.

Key **First** as a Name. Select **Normal** (from the pull-down menu) as **Style for following paragraph,** and be sure that **Normal** is there as **Style based on.** Change the radio button from **Only in this document** to **New documents based on this template.** Make sure **Add to Quick Style list** is checked.

```
Create New Style from Formatting                                    ᵇ  ⛌

  Properties
    Name:                         Style 1
    Style type:                   Paragraph                              ▾
    Style based on:               ¶ Normal                               ▾
    Style for following paragraph: ¶ Style 1                             ▾

  Formatting
    Palatino Linotype  ▾  11  ▾  B  I  U     Automatic  ▾

    ≣  ≣  ≣  ▣   =  =  ≡    ⌸  ⌸  ⌷  ⌷

    ┌─────────────────────────────────────────────────────────────┐
    │     Key First as a Name. Select Normal from the pull-down menu│
    │ as "style for following paragraph"—and be sure that Normal is │
    │ there as "style based on." Change the radio button from "Only │
    │ in this document" to "New documents based on this template."  │
    │ Make sure                                                     │
    │                                                               │
    └─────────────────────────────────────────────────────────────┘

    Style: Quick Style
      Based on: Normal

    ✓ Add to Quick Style list    ☐ Automatically update
    ◉ Only in this document        New documents based on this template

    Format ▾                              OK          Cancel
```

Figure 4.1 Creating a new style

Now click on **Format** and choose **Paragraph** from the pull-down menu, which yields the **Paragraph** dialog box. Change the **Special** setting from **First line** to **None** to turn off the paragraph indentation. Click **OK**, then **OK** again on the **Create New Style** dialog box.

The next time you save your document, Word will ask if you want to save changes to the template. You do. But first …

Automatic First Paragraphs

One more change will make things easier yet. Modify Heading 1 through Heading 4 (in each case, right-click on the name in the **Styles** palette and choose **Modify**) by changing **Style for following paragraph** from

Normal to First. In each case, make sure New documents based on this template is checked at the bottom of the dialog box. Now, when you type a heading and press Enter, the next paragraph will be a First paragraph rather than a Normal paragraph—and the next one after that will be back to Normal.

Letting Word Work For You

There are other settings you should check—certainly in every book template and probably in the default template:

➢ *Hyphenation*: If your book will use fully justified type, hyphenation should be on at the global level. Select the Page Layout tab, click on Hyphenation within Page Setup, and check Automatic. But you should also check Hyphenation Options to determine the maximum number of lines in a row that can have hyphens (two is the most you should allow) so as to avoid a column of hyphens. Now, modify Heading 1 and other Heading levels, choosing the Paragraph dialog box and the Line and Page Breaks section: Make sure Don't hyphenate is checked. (Keep with next and Keep lines together should also be checked. Widow/orphan control should be checked for all styles as a matter of course.)

➢ *Kerning*: Make sure Kerning for fonts is checked (on the Advanced tab in the Font dialog box) in all styles so that Word can space some pairs of letters (e.g., "Yo") properly. If it's checked in Normal and Heading 1, it should cascade to other styles. Usually, the default setting of 8 points is fine.

A Quick Introduction to Templates

If you haven't worked with templates before, this may seem a little confusing. Experiment with existing templates—there are dozens of them already on your computer or that you can download. Templates are powerful and are key to making Word do as much of your layout and typography work as possible:

➢ A template is a document you use to create other documents. It includes definitions for page size and margins, overall controls, and styles. It may also include graphics or text.

➢ Templates improve consistency and allow flexibility. If you use a style for a given type of heading, you know all the headings will look the same—and if you decide to change that look, you can change all of them at once.

➢ Some elements of a template work at the document level, some at the style (paragraph) level, some—including hyphenation—at both levels.

➢ Styles are cascading. Once you define a style as based on some other style, changes to the parent style will be reflected in the child style (unless the child style includes an override). So, as a primary example, if all body-text styles are based on Normal (as they should be) and all Heading styles that use a different type-face are based on Heading 1, you need only change the typeface in Normal or Heading 1 to change typeface usage throughout.

This chapter talks about picas and points and uses the pica as a standard unit of measurement. You may find it useful to change Word's defaults so that it shows picas and points. To do that, select the **File** tab, click on **Options** (near the bottom of the left side), click on **Advanced**, and scroll down to **Display**. The second item under **Display** is **Show measurements in units of.** Select **Picas** from the pull-down menu. That's it. From now on, the rulers and other meas-urements will appear in picas and points.

Elements of the Bk6pv Template

You *can* download book templates for various sized books from Lulu.com, but I'm not particularly impressed with what you get. Microsoft's own offerings don't include general-purpose book templates. That's why I've prepared two downloadable templates for readers of this book—with assistance from ITI—free to use, with no implied warranty as to fitness or quality.

Bk6pv.dotx, used to create this book, is available for download-ing at waltcrawford.name/bk6pv.dotx or by clicking the appropri-ate link at waltcrawford.name/lgm, the homepage for this book. Bk6pvex.dotx is an example template—it's based on bk6pv.dotx, but it adds sample text to show how things work and some front-matter sections, also as examples. If you're using a version of Word older than Word 2007, you'll also find links to bk6pv.dot and bk6pvex.dot at waltcrawford.name/lgm. Those templates should work with any Word back to Word 97.

Depending on your browser, you may find that clicking on either link opens Word—and if you've clicked on bk6pv.dotx, you'll be looking at an empty document. That's OK. Choose the File tab, click Save As, find Microsoft Word Template (.dotx) on the menu, and work with the directory pointer until you get to your username (from the desktop) and the folder hierarchy AppData, Roaming, Microsoft, Templates. Now you can save the template, and it will be one of your options when you click on New to create a new document.

What's in Bk6pv

At the page layout level, bk6pv.dotx defines the paper size as 36 picas wide and 54 picas high—in other words, 6" x 9". The top margin is 6 picas (with running headers 4 picas into that margin). The bottom margin is 56 points (4.67 picas) with the running footer, only on the first page of each chapter, 4 picas into that margin. There's a 4 pica margin on each side, with an additional 2 pica gutter to allow for binding. That means that odd-numbered (recto) pages have a 1" left margin while even-numbered (verso) pages have a 1" right margin.

The only text in bk6pv.dotx is baseline running headers and footers, which follow the most common style for nonfiction books. The first page of each new section (most commonly a chapter but also parts and special sections) has no header and a centered page number as a footer. Other even-numbered pages have no footer and have a left-aligned header consisting of the page number followed by the book name in italics: This appears as "*bookname*" in the template. Other odd-numbered pages have no footer and have a right-aligned header consisting of the chapter name in italics ("*chapname*" in the template) followed by the page number.

At the document level, hyphenation is automatic with a 1.5 pica zone and two line maximum.

These styles are defined, either modifying or in addition to dozens of built-in styles:

➢ *Normal*: Palatino Linotype 10 point type with exactly 13 point spacing, kerned at 8 points and above. No space above or below paragraph; special indent of 1 pica for the first line. (The 13 point spacing explains the 56 point bottom margin: Reducing that margin from 5 picas or 60 points fits exactly 40 lines of text on a page with no headings.)

➤ *First*: Same as Normal, but without the first-line indent.

➤ *Quote1*: Used for excerpted material longer than a sentence. This style uses Verdana 10 point type with exactly 12 point spacing, a 2 pica indent on both sides, and 6 point spacing above and below.

➤ *Quote2*: Like Quote1, but with 3 pica indents. Used rarely for quoted material *within* quoted material.

➤ *Heading 1*: Intended for chapter headings. 22 point Verdana (spacing exactly 24 points; large type doesn't require much extra vertical space), centered, with 48 points (4 picas) space above and 72 points (6 picas) space below. Heading 1 starts a new page—but you'll have to *explicitly* start a new section for the first-page footer to work correctly. (In this book, the chapter number itself is manually changed to 28 point.)

➤ *Heading 2*: 14 point Verdana **bold**, spacing exactly 16 points, 30 points (2.5 picas) space above, 6 points space below.

➤ *Heading 3*: 11 point Verdana, left aligned, spacing exactly 13 points, 20 points space above, 6 points space below.

➤ *Heading 4*: 11 point Verdana *italic*, left aligned, spacing exactly 13 points, 20 points space above, 6 points space below.

➤ *bibgloss*: Same as Normal, but with a hanging indent of 1.5 picas instead of a first-line indent of 1 pica and spacing of 6 points above and below. Intended for entries in bibliography or glossary.

➤ *bullet*: Like this paragraph: Normal type with a bullet and with 6 points space above and below each bullet.

➤ *Front*: Same as Heading 1, but set to Body text as an outline level, which means it won't generate a table of contents entry. Used for section headings in front matter (acknowledgments, foreword, etc.).

➤ *c1, c2, e1, e2*: Character styles to condense or expand selected type by 0.1 or 0.2, points respectively. Described further in Chapter 6.

These styles should only be used on full paragraphs that don't have italics or bold.

You may find other styles in this template, in addition to dozens of styles provided by Word (most of which can't be deleted). For example, the custom character style ui in bk6pvex.dotx switches selected text to Verdana, the typeface used in this book for portions of user interfaces.

Bk6pvex.dotx is based on bk6pv.dotx but adds a sample title page, copyright page, table of contents, and two chapters with sample text as examples of how the template works. If you download this template, you should see text—and if you want to use this template for your own book, make sure to delete the sample text.

Modifying the Template

The templates provided represent starting points. This book uses bk6pv.dotx (more specifically bk6pvex.dotx), and the combination of Palatino and Verdana appears suitable for a wide range of books (and includes typefaces with full or nearly full kerning).

You may want to customize your book template. If you do so, I'd suggest saving the new template with a different name for clarity (using Save as with Word template [.dotx] selected from the pull-down in Save as). So, for example, if you prefer Garamond to Palatino but want to identify the template as being for a 6" x 9" book, bk6gv.dotx might be a plausible template name.

The next chapter considers some of your choices when modifying a template. Key reminders are:

➢ Modify Normal if you're changing body typeface or size. That will change the typeface in all body styles except Quote1 and Quote2 (although you may need to check body styles for size changes).

➢ Modify Heading 1 if you're changing heading/display typeface or size. That will change the typeface in Front, Heading 2, Heading 3, and Heading 4, but you'll have to check the other styles for size.

➢ If you're changing the line spacing to something other than 13 points, you'll want to tweak the bottom margin and spacing around headings in order to minimize overall spacing issues.

Alternative Approaches

If you don't have Word, there's also a LibreOffice/OpenOffice template at waltcrawford.name/bk6lb.ott. I find template handling and typography in general somewhat clumsier in LibreOffice, but it's there if you want it, along with two chapters of sample text.

Key differences are:

➢ Because Linux and LibreOffice, when installed on computers that don't have Microsoft Office, may be lacking in popular typeface families, I've used Lucida Bright for body text and Lucida Sans for headings.

➢ I was unable to see how to start new chapters as new Sections and have the first page running headers and footers different from other left and right pages, so I've used a simplified running header and footer: centered book title as a running header on all pages, centered page number as a running footer on all pages. You should try to suppress the book title on the first page of each chapter if you can do so.

Otherwise, style and page definitions are comparable to those in bk6pv.dotx.

The Basics

Whether you're starting a new template or modifying an existing one, you should check several things to ensure that Word (or LibreOffice) automates as much as possible of the task of making your book presentable. Some of the basics are:

➢ *Widow/Orphan control* (on the Line and page breaks tab of the Paragraph dialog box) should *always* be on. Widows and orphans are stranded lines of paragraphs—that is, where the last line of a multiline paragraph is at the top of a page or the first line of a multiline paragraph is at the bottom of a page. That should never happen. Note that this Word control does *not* prevent the other category of orphans, parts of words or short single words appearing as the last line of a paragraph.

➢ *For headings only*, three other options on the Line and page breaks tab should always be checked: Keep with next (so the heading doesn't appear at the bottom of one page with the paragraph starting on the next page), **Keep lines together** (multiline headings shouldn't break across pages), and **Don't hyphenate** (headings should never be hyphenated). You also want to make sure heading styles are never fully justified.

➤ *Kerning for fonts* on the **Advanced** tab of the **Paragraph** dialog box should almost always be checked, with the default point value usually acceptable (or just use 8 points in all cases). You'll see in the next chapter what kerning does.

➤ Base text styles on Normal and heading styles on Heading 1 (or Normal, if they're headings that use the body typeface), so that changes in typeface cascade through other styles.

Just a Starting Point

The bk6pv.dotx template will yield well-balanced nonfiction books—or fiction books, for that matter, although fiction rarely uses any headings below the chapter level. That template was used for this book.

But it's just a starting point. If you'd like a different look for your book, if you prefer other typefaces, if you find the type too small, if you think you'd like a little more air between lines within a paragraph, or if you need to use different size pages, you should build a new template. You should look at the results—at least a page or two of printed examples—and have other people offer advice. Are the heading levels clear? Do the body and heading typefaces work well together?

The next chapter shows some of your options. Using this book's template as a starting point, you can build hundreds of different templates with very little effort and without making any extreme choices.

5
Typography and Layout

This chapter contains many examples of typefaces, type sizes, line spacing, kerning, and justification. The first section provides the principles and most common situations. You may find that's all you need. Those of you with a real eye for layout may notice one difference between this chapter and the others: Example paragraphs are neither condensed nor expanded except as explicitly noted, which may result in some larger-than-usual spaces between paragraphs.

Basics and Norms

Most books use a serif typeface for text—a typeface with added details at the ends of some strokes, such as the horizontal bars at the tops and bottoms of the outside strokes in "M." Readability studies have consistently shown that serif typefaces are easier to read in long textual passages, especially in high-resolution print. Many books, including this one, use sans serif typefaces for most headings in order to provide contrast.

Your choice of typeface should depend on what's available to you and your own judgment (aided by other sets of eyes and tastes)—but it's also true that some typefaces take up more space than others. Later in this chapter, you'll find examples of serif typeface families normally available with Windows 7. You may once have had Office 2007 or Word 2007 on your computer, and it's possible you are still using them. If so, you have several more good candidates for body typefaces, including some classic typefaces, with examples later in this chapter. (Microsoft cut back on typeface support for Office 2010, which doesn't add new typefaces. Fortunately, the typefaces already installed on your computer stay there unless you explicitly delete them.) You'll also find brief examples of some sans serif typefaces that might be suitable for headings and subheading in typical books.

Size

Most books use body type set at 10 points, 11 points, or 12 points (the point measure being the height of the tallest letters). This book uses 10 point type because Palatino Linotype sets larger than some other type-faces—that is, letters are a little bigger. Type smaller than 9 points (frequently used in magazines and newspapers) starts to get into the want ad and fine-print categories; type larger than 12 points is mostly used for headings and signs, with the exception of large-print books, which typically use 16 point type.

Why would you want to change from 10 point type? If you select another typeface, you may find that it's a little small at 10 points. If you're doing an 8.5" x 11" book with a single column of text (which you might do in order to insert lots of photographs or family group sheets in a family history, for example), increasing the body type to 11 or 12 points is one way to deal with very long lines of type.

Spacing or Leading

Typographers refer to additional space between lines within a para-graph as *leading* because it was originally added by inserting thin strips of lead. Word calls this Line spacing. In both cases, the number used is the *total* space from the bottom of one line to the bottom of the line below it—not the added space itself. You may see the combination of type size and leading referred to as "X over Y" (e.g., "10 over 13" for 10 point type on 13 point line spacing, as used in this book).

The most common text leading is 20 percent to 30 percent—10 point type spaced at 12 or 13 points, 11 over 13 or 14, 12 over 14 or 15. You can modify that, but look carefully at the consequences. It's difficult to reduce line spacing much below 20 percent without mak-ing the text feel crowded. If you have very wide lines (again, as in the 8.5" x 11" book), some extra spacing might be worthwhile—but anything much beyond 40 percent begins to look funny and may appear as though you're trying to make a short text more impressive by spacing it out.

Word offers two ways to specify line spacing: Exactly and At least. This book and the bk6pv.dotx template use exact line spacing because it provides better control. At least will increase line spacing for some typefaces and some uses of text. It may provide a better look, but it decreases your control over layout. (In the case of Palatino Linotype, for example, using 11 point type on "at least 13 point" line spacing apparently results in 14 or 15 point line spacing.)

Multiline headings larger than about 16 points typically do not require 20 percent line spacing. For example, Heading 1 in this book (and the bk6pv.dotx template) has the line spacing set only 10 percent larger than the type size, and, when using larger type, I've sometimes found it useful to set line spacing to the same as or even less than the type size, counterintuitive as that might seem.

Justification and Hyphenation

If you don't justify, don't hyphenate. That may be too crude a rule, but it's a good starting point. If you *do* hyphenate, don't allow too many hyphenated lines in a row. I limit them to two lines at a time and recommend that you do the same, as even three hyphenated lines in a row can be distracting.

Should you justify? Most books—I'd guess at least 90 percent of fiction and nonfiction books published in America—are fully justified, with the right edge of each paragraph lined up neatly. Many of us feel that justified text looks a little more polished and finished. On the other hand, some publishers think justified text is old-fashioned and prefer left-aligned unjustified text. You can certainly choose left-aligned unjustified text for your book; after all, it is your book. That will eliminate awkward wide spaces when you have long words or URLs on a line that don't hyphenate well.

I can't think of any cases in which body text in a book should be centered or right aligned. On the other hand, an epigraph at the start of a chapter might work well right aligned, and there may be other special cases in which specific kinds of text could be effective with right alignment.

Headings are different. They should never be hyphenated, and they should never be justified. This book uses centered headings for the first level and left-aligned headings for other levels, but you might try using right-aligned headings for chapter titles, as one example.

Ligatures

New (for Windows) in Office 2010 (although a feature of advanced typesetting for many years), ligatures combine two letters (e.g., ff and fi) into a single, better-looking combination or provide other joins or flourishes based on context.

While bk6pv.dotx has ligature support turned on for standard and contextual ligatures—but not a broader range of historical ligatures—that's meaningless for most standard typefaces, as they don't include the OpenType characteristics to support ligatures.

If you're using a typeface that can support ligatures and if you're doing the right kind of book (e.g., a historical memoir), you might want to expand the use of ligatures to include all available. Let taste and good advice be your guides. Where a typeface appears to support more than minimal ligatures in the examples that follow, it is noted. (Note that ligatures may cause problems in spell-check or indexing.)

Those are the basics. Now let's look at examples of what's available on a typical computer running Windows 7—and the broader range available if you use Office 2007 or previously had it or Word 2007 installed on your computer.

Choosing a Typeface for the Body

When choosing a typeface, consider the nature of your book and the "feel" that seems best to you. While this template uses Palatino Linotype (usually called Palatino), I find Constantia to be a particularly nice text typeface, and you may prefer something else.

Typefaces differ in the amount of space they require for a given amount of copy, although the typefaces available in Windows 7 are all within a narrow range. Californian FB, Garamond, Goudy Old Style, and Perpetua are all relatively compact; Bookman Old Style, Century Schoolbook, and Lucida Bright will require significantly more space. At the extremes, a book that's 140 pages in Perpetua might be 200 pages in Lucida Bright.

Try the typeface you like over several pages. Try different printers if you have them—and using the draft mode for a printer may expose weaknesses in a typeface. Show the results to others, especially if you know people who are sensitive to typography. Every typeface shown so far can yield handsome, readable books, but they do vary.

Thinking About the Samples

Which of the typefaces seems most readable as a paragraph? Which do you find cramped? Do you find some of them starting to fall apart as paragraphs because there's too much white space?

To my eye, Palatino with less than 20 percent line spacing is cramped, and 30 percent looks better. If I were producing an 8.5" x 11" book, I'd probably use 30 percent and possibly 40 percent spacing and might change to 12 point type; more than 40 percent, and you're using a lot of extra space and possibly losing paragraph integrity. If you're using a different typeface, especially one that's smaller or larger than usual, try some multipage samples in print form before making a final decision—but in general, the 20 percent to 30 percent spacing rule works well.

One word on the samples: While normal layout rules for ITI preclude breaking words across lines with only two letters on one line, these samples ignore that particular rule.

Typeface Families: Windows 7

The examples that follow show the same text in each of the typeface families you should already have as part of Windows 7. I say "typeface families" because each of these has at least roman, bold, and italic versions, and usually bold italic as well. Bold and italic effects produced by modifying an existing typeface never look as good as the real thing. Each paragraph is set 10 over 13, which may not be the best combination for some of these typefaces. I've added notes in a few cases. Almost all of these typefaces were also distributed with Windows Vista as well as Windows 7. Except as noted, each of these families has very good or excellent kerning support.

Windows 7 also comes with Georgia, a good typeface family that appears to lack most or all kerning information, making it a less useful choice for books.

Cambria

The Quick Brown Fox Jumped Over the Lazy Dog. 1&2#3$4%5 6?7 "89". Kerning and ligatures: Tam's AV Was Void—finally and officially cast out.

The Quick Brown Fox Jumped Over the Lazy Dog. 1&2#3$4%5 6?7 "89".
Kerning and ligatures: Tam's AV Was Void—finally and officially cast out.
The Quick Brown Fox Jumped Over the Lazy Dog. 1&2#3$4%5 6?7
"89". Kerning and ligatures: Tam's AV Was Void—finally and official-
ly cast out. Ours is a noble old house, and stretches a long way back into
antiquity. The earliest ancestor the Twains have any record of was a
friend of the family by the name of Higgins. [*Mark Twain's (Burlesque)*
Auto-Biography via Project Gutenberg]

Constantia

The Quick Brown Fox Jumped Over the Lazy Dog. 1&2#3$4%5 6?7 "89".
Kerning and ligatures: Tam's AV Was Void—finally and officially cast out.
The Quick Brown Fox Jumped Over the Lazy Dog. 1&2#3$4%5 6?7 "89".
Kerning and ligatures: Tam's AV Was Void—finally and officially cast out.
The Quick Brown Fox Jumped Over the Lazy Dog. 1&2#3$4%5 6?7
"89". Kerning and ligatures: Tam's AV Was Void—finally and offi-
cially cast out. Ours is a noble old house, and stretches a long way back
into antiquity. The earliest ancestor the Twains have any record of was a
friend of the family by the name of Higgins. [*Mark Twain's (Burlesque)*
Auto-Biography via Project Gutenberg]

Note the "fi" ligature here.

Palatino Linotype

The Quick Brown Fox Jumped Over the Lazy Dog. 1&2#3$4%5 6?7
"89". Kerning and ligatures: Tam's AV Was Void—finally and officially cast out. *The Quick Brown Fox Jumped Over the Lazy Dog. 1&2#3$4%5*
6?7 "89". Kerning and ligatures: Tam's AV Was Void—finally and officially
cast out. **The Quick Brown Fox Jumped Over the Lazy Dog.**
1&2#3$4%5 6?7 "89". Kerning and ligatures: Tam's AV Was Void—
finally and officially cast out. Ours is a noble old house, and stretches
a long way back into antiquity. The earliest ancestor the Twains have
any record of was a friend of the family by the name of Higgins. [*Mark*
Twain's (Burlesque) Auto-Biography via Project Gutenberg]

Palatino Linotype, used in this book and in bk6pv.dotx, is slightly lacking in kerning information. The type sample above is set to show *all* ligatures and special forms: Note the "st" combination and the capital Q in

the example. The template has only standard and contextual ligatures and special forms enabled, probably appropriate for most modern books.

Times New Roman

The Quick Brown Fox Jumped Over the Lazy Dog. 1&2#3$4%5 6?7 "89". Kerning and ligatures: Tam's AV Was Void—finally and officially cast out. *The Quick Brown Fox Jumped Over the Lazy Dog. 1&2#3$4%5 6?7 "89". Kerning and ligatures: Tam's AV Was Void—finally and officially cast out.* **The Quick Brown Fox Jumped Over the Lazy Dog. 1&2#3$4%5 6?7 "89". Kerning and ligatures: Tam's AV Was Void—finally and officially cast out**. Ours is a noble old house, and stretches a long way back into antiquity. The earliest ancestor the Twains have any record of was a friend of the family by the name of Higgins. [*Mark Twain's (Burlesque) Auto-Biography* via Project Gutenberg]

Text Families: Microsoft Office 2007

If you've ever had Word 2007 or Office 2007 on your computer, you should have a broader range of typefaces, including some classic text families. One word of caution: Some classic typefaces with thin letterforms may not print as reliably with the high-speed laser printers used by Lulu and CreateSpace. If printed samples seem "thin," these typefaces may not be ideal choices.

You also have some other text families that appear to lack kerning information entirely, such as Book Antiqua, Bookman Old Style, Californian FB, and Century Schoolbook. Some of these are attractive, if you don't mind the loss of kerning. Try extended samples before using these typefaces. You'll also find some serif typefaces that are "singletons"—they lack italic and bold versions. I wouldn't use those for books: While Word will slant text for an italic look, it's a bad substitute for actual italic design. (An easy way to see whether an italic is a true italic: With very few exceptions—a few under-designed sans serif typefaces—the lowercase "a" becomes a simplified "*a*" with no upper curve.)

Bodoni MT

The Quick Brown Fox Jumped Over the Lazy Dog. 1&2#3$4%5 6?7 "89". Kerning: Tam's AV Was Void—finally and officially cast out. *The Quick*

Brown Fox Jumped Over the Lazy Dog. **The Quick Brown Fox Jumped Over the Lazy Dog.** Ours is a noble old house, and stretches a long way back into antiquity. The earliest ancestor the Twains have any record of was a friend of the family by the name of Higgins. [*Mark Twain's (Burlesque) Auto-Biography* via Project Gutenberg]

Calisto MT

The Quick Brown Fox Jumped Over the Lazy Dog. 1&2#3$4%5 6?7 "89". Kerning: Tam's AV Was Void—finally and officially cast out. *The Quick Brown Fox Jumped Over the Lazy Dog.* **The Quick Brown Fox Jumped Over the Lazy Dog.** Ours is a noble old house, and stretches a long way back into antiquity. The earliest ancestor the Twains have any record of was a friend of the family by the name of Higgins. [*Mark Twain's (Burlesque) Auto-Biography* via Project Gutenberg]

Garamond

The Quick Brown Fox Jumped Over the Lazy Dog. 1&2#3$4%5 6?7 "89". Kerning: Tam's AV Was Void—finally and officially cast out. *The Quick Brown Fox Jumped Over the Lazy Dog.* **The Quick Brown Fox Jumped Over the Lazy Dog.** Ours is a noble old house, and stretches a long way back into antiquity. The earliest ancestor the Twains have any record of was a friend of the family by the name of Higgins. [*Mark Twain's (Burlesque) Auto-Biography* via Project Gutenberg]

Goudy Old Style

The Quick Brown Fox Jumped Over the Lazy Dog. 1&2#3$4%5 6?7 "89". Kerning: Tam's AV Was Void–finally and officially cast out. *The Quick Brown Fox Jumped Over the Lazy Dog.* **The Quick Brown Fox Jumped Over the Lazy Dog.** Ours is a noble old house, and stretches a long way back into antiquity. The earliest ancestor the Twains have any record of was a friend of the family by the name of Higgins. [*Mark Twain's (Burlesque) Auto-Biography* via Project Gutenberg]

Lucida Bright

The Quick Brown Fox Jumped Over the Lazy Dog. 1&2#3$4%5 6?7 "89". Kerning: Tam's AV Was Void—finally and officially cast out. *The Quick Brown Fox Jumped Over the Lazy Dog.* **The Quick Brown Fox Jumped Over the Lazy Dog.** Ours is a noble old house, and stretches a long way back into antiquity. The earliest ancestor the Twains have any record of was a friend of the family by the name of Higgins. [*Mark Twain's (Burlesque) Auto-Biography* via Project Gutenberg]

This typeface has incomplete kerning information.

Perpetua

The Quick Brown Fox Jumped Over the Lazy Dog. 1&2#3$4%5 6?7 "89". Kerning: Tam's AV Was Void—finally and officially cast out. *The Quick Brown Fox Jumped Over the Lazy Dog.* **The Quick Brown Fox Jumped Over the Lazy Dog.** Ours is a noble old house, and stretches a long way back into antiquity. The earliest ancestor the Twains have any record of was a friend of the family by the name of Higgins. [*Mark Twain's (Burlesque) Auto-Biography* via Project Gutenberg]

Size and Spacing

The following examples show a range of type size and spacing options. Consider both legibility (how easy it is to read letters) and readability (how easy it is to read the stream of text)—but also note that these factors will change on very wide or very narrow lines. (The text in these examples is one remarkable sentence from Project Gutenberg's transcription of a facsimile edition of Lewis Carroll's handwritten version of *Alice's Adventures Under Ground*, which later became *Alice's Adventures in Wonderland*.) All examples use Palatino Linotype.

10 Point Type on 10 Point Spacing

Hardly knowing what she did, she picked up a little bit of stick, and held it out to the puppy: whereupon the puppy jumped into the air off all its feet at once, and with a yelp of delight rushed at the stick, and made believe to worry it then Alice dodged behind a great thistle to keep herself from being run over, and, the moment she appeared at the other side, the puppy made another dart at the stick, and tumbled head over heels in its hurry to get hold: then Alice, thinking it was very like having a game of play with a cart-horse, and expecting every moment to be trampled under its feet, ran round the thistle again: then the puppy begin a series of short charges at the stick, running a very little way forwards each time and a long way back, and barking hoarsely all the while, till at last it sat down a good way off, panting, with its tongue hanging out of its mouth, and its great eyes half shut.

10 Point Type on 12 Point ("Single") Spacing (Typical)

Hardly knowing what she did, she picked up a little bit of stick, and held it out to the puppy: whereupon the puppy jumped into the air off all its feet at once, and with a yelp of delight rushed at the stick, and made believe to worry it then Alice dodged behind a great thistle to keep herself from being run over, and, the moment she appeared at the other side, the puppy made another dart at the stick, and tumbled head over heels in its hurry to get hold: then Alice, thinking it was very like having a game of play with a cart-horse, and expecting every moment to be trampled under its feet, ran round the thistle again: then the puppy begin a series of short charges at the stick, running a very little way forwards each time and a long way back, and barking hoarsely all the while, till at last it sat down a good way off, panting, with its tongue hanging out of its mouth, and its great eyes half shut.

10 Point Type on 14 Point Spacing

Hardly knowing what she did, she picked up a little bit of stick, and held it out to the puppy: whereupon the puppy jumped into the air off all its feet at once, and with a yelp of delight rushed at the stick, and made believe to worry it then Alice dodged behind a great thistle to keep herself from being run over, and, the moment she appeared at the other side, the puppy made another dart at the stick, and tumbled head over heels in its hurry to get hold: then Alice, thinking it was very like having a game of play with a cart-horse, and expecting every moment to be trampled under its feet, ran round the thistle again: then the puppy begin a series of short charges at the stick, running a very little way forwards each time and a long way back, and barking hoarsely all the while, till at last it sat down a good way off, panting, with its tongue hanging out of its mouth, and its great eyes half shut.

10 Point Type on 16 Point Spacing

Hardly knowing what she did, she picked up a little bit of stick, and held it out to the puppy: whereupon the puppy jumped into the air off all its feet at once, and with a yelp of delight rushed at the stick, and made believe to worry it then Alice dodged behind a great thistle to keep herself from being run over, and, the moment she appeared at the other side, the puppy made another dart at the stick, and tumbled head over heels in its hurry to get hold: then Alice, thinking it was very like having a game of play with a cart-horse, and expecting every moment to be trampled under its feet, ran round the thistle again: then the puppy begin a series of short charges at the stick, running a very little way forwards each time and a long way back, and barking hoarsely all the while, till at last it sat down a good way off, panting, with its tongue hanging out of its mouth, and its great eyes half shut.

11 Point Type on 12 Point Spacing

Hardly knowing what she did, she picked up a little bit of stick, and held it out to the puppy: whereupon the puppy jumped into the air off all its feet at once, and with a yelp of delight rushed at the stick, and made believe to worry it then Alice dodged behind a great thistle to keep herself from being run over, and, the moment she appeared at the other side, the puppy made another dart at the stick, and tumbled head over heels in its hurry to get hold: then Alice, thinking it was very like having a game of play with a cart-horse, and expecting every moment to be trampled under its feet, ran round the thistle again: then the puppy begin a series of short charges at the stick, running a very little way forwards each time and a long way back, and barking hoarsely all the while, till at last it sat down a good way off, panting, with its tongue hanging out of its mouth, and its great eyes half shut.

11 Point Type on "At Least 13"

Hardly knowing what she did, she picked up a little bit of stick, and held it out to the puppy: whereupon the puppy jumped into the air off all its feet at once, and with a yelp of delight rushed at the stick, and made believe to worry it then Alice dodged behind a great thistle to keep herself from being run over, and, the moment she appeared at the other side, the puppy made another dart at the stick, and tumbled head over heels in its hurry to get hold: then Alice, thinking it was very like having a game of play with a cart-horse, and expecting every moment to be trampled under its feet, ran round the thistle again: then the puppy begin a series of short charges at the stick, running a very little way forwards each time and a long way back, and barking hoarsely all the while, till at last it sat down a good way off, panting, with its tongue hanging out of its mouth, and its great eyes half shut.

11 Point Type on 15 Point Spacing

Hardly knowing what she did, she picked up a little bit of stick, and held it out to the puppy: whereupon the puppy jumped into the air off all its feet at once, and with a yelp of delight rushed at the stick, and made believe to worry it then Alice dodged behind a great thistle to keep herself from being run over, and, the moment she appeared at the other side, the puppy made another dart at the stick, and tumbled head over heels in its hurry to get hold: then Alice, thinking it was very like having a game of play with a cart-horse, and expecting every moment to be trampled under its feet, ran round the thistle again: then the puppy begin a series of short charges at the stick, running a very little way forwards each time and a long way back, and barking hoarsely all the while, till at last it sat down a good way off, panting, with its tongue hanging out of its mouth, and its great eyes half shut.

12 Point Type on 13 Point Spacing

Hardly knowing what she did, she picked up a little bit of stick, and held it out to the puppy: whereupon the puppy jumped into the air off all its feet at once, and with a yelp of delight rushed at the stick, and made believe to worry it then Alice dodged behind a great thistle to keep herself from being run over, and, the moment she appeared at the other side, the puppy made another dart at the stick, and tumbled head over heels in its hurry to get hold: then Alice, thinking it was very like having a game of play with a cart-horse, and expecting every moment to be trampled under its feet, ran round the thistle again: then the puppy begin a series of short charges at the stick, running a very little way forwards each time and a long way back, and barking hoarsely all the while, till at last it sat down a good way off, panting, with its tongue hanging out of its mouth, and its great eyes half shut.

12 Point Type on 15 Point Spacing

Hardly knowing what she did, she picked up a little bit of stick, and held it out to the puppy: whereupon the puppy jumped into the air off all its feet at once, and with a yelp of delight rushed at the stick, and made believe to worry it then Alice dodged behind a great thistle to keep herself from being run over, and, the moment she appeared at the other side, the puppy made another dart at the stick, and tumbled head over heels in its hurry to get hold: then Alice, thinking it was very like having a game of play with a cart-horse, and expecting every moment to be trampled under its feet, ran round the thistle again: then the puppy begin a series of short charges at the stick, running a very little way forwards each time and a long way back, and barking hoarsely all the while, till at last it sat down a good way off, panting, with its tongue hanging out of its mouth, and its great eyes half shut.

12 Point Type on 17 Point Spacing

Hardly knowing what she did, she picked up a little bit of stick, and held it out to the puppy: whereupon the puppy jumped into the air off all its feet at once, and with a yelp of delight rushed at the stick, and made believe to worry it then Alice dodged behind a great thistle to keep herself from being run over, and, the moment she appeared at the other side, the puppy made another dart at the stick, and tumbled head over heels in its hurry to get hold: then Alice, thinking it was very like having a game of play with a cart-horse, and expecting every moment to be trampled under its feet, ran round the thistle again: then the puppy begin a series of short charges at the stick, running a very little way forwards each time and a long way back, and barking hoarsely all the while, till at last it sat down a good way off, panting, with its tongue hanging out of its mouth, and its great eyes half shut.

16 Point Type on 20 Point Spacing: Large Print

Hardly knowing what she did, she picked up a little bit of stick, and held it out to the puppy: whereupon the puppy jumped into the air off all its feet at once, and with a yelp of delight rushed at the stick, and made believe to worry it then Alice dodged behind a great thistle to keep herself from being run over, and, the moment she appeared at the other side, the puppy made another dart at the stick, and tumbled head over heels in its hurry to get hold: then Alice, thinking it was very like having a game of play with a cart-horse, and expecting every moment to be trampled under its feet, ran round the thistle again: then the puppy begin a series of short charges at the stick, running a very little way forwards each time and a long way back, and barking hoarsely all the while, till at last it sat down a good way off, panting, with its tongue hanging out of its mouth, and its great eyes half shut.

While 16 point type on 19 point lines is the most common large print specification, this example uses 16 over 20 because of Palatino Linotype's size.

Justification and Hyphenation

You're so unlikely to ever use centered or right-aligned body text in a book that I don't think there's much point in showing examples, but here's the sample sentence set flush left and without hyphenation, since that's a reasonable alternative

10 Point on 13, Left Aligned, No Hyphenation

Hardly knowing what she did, she picked up a little bit of stick, and held it out to the puppy: whereupon the puppy jumped into the air off all its feet at once, and with a yelp of delight rushed at the stick, and made believe to worry it then Alice dodged behind a great thistle to keep herself from being run over, and, the moment she appeared at the other side, the puppy made another dart at the stick, and tumbled head over heels in its hurry to get hold: then Alice, thinking it was very like having a game of play with a cart-horse, and expecting every moment to be trampled under its feet, ran round the thistle again: then the puppy begin a series of short charges at the stick, running a very little way forwards each time and a long way back, and barking hoarsely all the while, till at last it sat down a good way off, panting, with its tongue hanging out of its mouth, and its great eyes half shut.

Choosing a Typeface for Headings

You can use the same typeface family for body text and headings, but you probably won't. If you use a different headings typeface, it should almost certainly be a sans serif or semi serif typeface. There are too many possibilities to offer samples of here, but the following are some sans serif *families* that should be on your computer and probably aren't too extreme to use as book headings.

There are many other reasonable options. You might want unusual headings. For example, a book containing family diaries might look great with headings set in a "handwriting" typeface such as Bradley Hand ITC.

Basic Options

The brief examples of heading typefaces that follow are in 16 point type on 18 point spacing, left aligned, with kerning active (most of these are kerned) and ligatures active. Calibri has an extensive set of ligatures and contextual alternatives and is shown with all of them turned on (note the "ck" combination).

Arial

The Quick Brown Fox Jumped Over the final Lazy Dog To Yo Wa Ve AV 1! 2@ 3# 4$ 5% 6^ 7& 8* 9 (0) {}

Calibri

The Quick Brown Fox Jumped Over the final Lazy Dog To Yo Wa Ve AV 1! 2@ 3# 4$ 5% 6^ 7& 8* 9 (0) {}

Candara

The Quick Brown Fox Jumped Over the final Lazy Dog To Yo Wa Ve AV 1! 2@ 3# 4$ 5% 6^ 7& 8* 9 (0) {}

Corbel

The Quick Brown Fox Jumped Over the final Lazy Dog To Yo Wa Ve AV 1! 2@ 3# 4$ 5% 6^ 7& 8* 9 (0) {}

Lucida Sans

The Quick Brown Fox Jumped Over the final Lazy Dog To Yo Wa Ve AV 1! 2@ 3# 4$ 5% 6^ 7& 8* 9 (0) {}

Segoe UI

The Quick Brown Fox Jumped Over the final Lazy Dog To Yo Wa Ve AV 1! 2@ 3# 4$ 5% 6^ 7& 8* 9 (0) {}

Tahoma

The Quick Brown Fox Jumped Over the final Lazy Dog To Yo Wa Ve AV 1! 2@ 3# 4$ 5% 6^ 7& 8* 9 (0) {}

Trebuchet MS

The Quick Brown Fox Jumped Over the final Lazy Dog To Yo Wa Ve AV 1! 2@ 3# 4$ 5% 6^ 7& 8* 9 (0) {}

Verdana

The Quick Brown Fox Jumped Over the final Lazy Dog To Yo Wa Ve AV 1! 2@ 3# 4$ 5% 6^ 7& 8* 9 (0) {}

Special Cases

You might find a specialty display typeface suitable for headings in an unusual book, and there are professional publishers who use distinctive heading typefaces as part of a corporate look. I'd be cautious about using any of the following, but under the right circumstances, they could work. These examples are set 16 on 18, similar to the heading typefaces just shown.

Agency FB

The Quick Brown Fox Jumped Over the final Lazy Dog To Yo Wa Ve AV 1! 2@ 3# 4$ 5% 6^ 7& 8* 9 (0) {}

Algerian

THE QUICK BROWN FOX JUMPED OVER THE FINAL LAZY DOG TO YO WA VE AV 1! 2@ 3# 4$ 5% 6^ 7& 8* 9 (0) {}

Blackadder ITC

The Quick Brown Fox Jumped Over the final Lazy Dog
To Yo Wa Ve AV 1! 2@ 3# 4$ 5% 6^ 7& 8* 9 (o) {}

Bradley Hand ITC

The Quick Brown Fox Jumped Over the final
Lazy Dog To Yo Wa Ve AV 1! 2@ 3# 4$ 5%
6 ^ 7& 8* 9 (0) {}

Broadway

The Quick Brown Fox Jumped Over the final Lazy Dog To Yo Wa Ve AV 1! 2@ 3# 4$ 5% 6^ 7& 8* 9 (0) { }

Gabriola

The Quick Brown Fox Jumped Over the final Lazy Dog To Yo Wa
Ve AV 1! 2@ 3# 4$ 5% 6^ 7& 8* 9 (0) {}

Nyala

The Quick Brown Fox Jumped Over the final Lazy
Dog To Yo Wa Ve AV 1! 2@ 3# 4$ 5% 6^ 7& 8* 9 (0)
{}

Other Considerations for Headings

Once again, you can be more flexible with headings. This book uses centered chapter headings at 22 points, left-aligned 14 point headings (Heading 2) within chapters, left-aligned 11 point bold subheadings (Heading 3), but you could just as easily use right-aligned chapter headings (I've seen it done in handsome books), and headings within chapters could be centered, all caps, or boldface upper-lower.

Look for balance and ease of maintenance. Heading 1 should always be significantly larger than Heading 2; Heading 2 should always be larger than Heading 3; Heading 3 should be bolder than Heading 4. Otherwise, as long as it enhances the book you're working on, you should experiment with heading typefaces and typography until you like what you see.

6
Making It Look Better

At this point, you have a book template that suits your own preferences. Widow and orphan control is always on. Typefaces are always kerned. Headings are always kept together and kept with the following paragraph.

You've written and edited your book, either working in the book template as you go or inserting the existing chapters into a new document based on the book template—and changed each paragraph following a heading to First. You've gotten feedback from others (or reviewed the text carefully yourself), and you're happy with the text.

You now have a book that probably looks as good as most that come from vanity publishers and quite a few that come from traditional publishers and self-publishers. But you can do a *lot* better.

Yes, it's true that your book hasn't had the individualized expert attention a professional designer can provide, that you don't have the huge range of typefaces available to a professional designer, and that your book will be produced using laser printing, not offset or letterpress printing. All or any of those factors could result in a book that looks less polished. However, this chapter provides detailed instructions for other techniques you *can* take to make your book look better.

The techniques in this chapter, which don't take much time to apply, will help make your book look as good as it can, adding professional polish to your micropublication. While the processes discussed here may include tiny editorial changes, they should typically be the very last thing you do before indexing, updating the table of contents, and generating a PDF. The steps discussed in this chapter are steps *not* taken for a lot of books from the biggest publishing houses (in one random sample of recent books, three-quarters showed signs

69

of problems that these steps will resolve), but they're steps that are worth taking.

Bad Breaks and Copyfitting

Bad breaks fall into a few categories, not including awkward and incorrect hyphenation:

1. Widows: Last lines of paragraphs appearing at the very top of a page.
2. Orphaned lines: First lines of paragraphs appearing at the very bottom of a page. Typographers also use orphan to refer to last lines of paragraphs consisting of one short word or part of a word; for this discussion, I'm including such orphans as the final category of bad breaks, since you'll use a different techniques to prevent them.
3. Stranded headings: Headings appearing at the very bottom of a page, separated from the first paragraph below the heading.
4. Orphaned words: Last lines of paragraphs consisting of part of a word or a relatively short word.

You've already prevented widows and orphaned lines (using **Widow/Orphan Control**) as well as stranded headings (using **Keep with next** and **Keep lines together**). However, preventing orphaned words or parts of words as the last line of a paragraph is a little trickier and can involve some combination of editing and copyfitting.

Copyfitting? The proper definition has to do with assuring that a given block of text fits within an allotted space. Here's a more specialized meaning: adjusting text so that you avoid orphaned words.

The Problem

You have a paragraph with a short last line—just one word or part of a word. You'll have to define "short" for yourself; I'd say "no more than seven characters," but you might take that down to as few as five characters. That short line looks bad and, when there are quite a few of them, makes your book longer than it needs to be.

That last is not a hypothetical. When I'm working on my ejournal, *Cites & Insights*, I always have a goal of making the issue fill an even number of pages. I get there by a combination of techniques, but I've found that copyfitting alone—eliminating short last lines of paragraphs—can take a 35-page draft down to 32 pages.

You probably shouldn't try to fix bad breaks for very short paragraphs; it may not be feasible without rewording or extreme changes. I'd suggest that any paragraph at least four lines long (including a bad break) is a good candidate for copyfitting.

Possible Solutions

You could change your wording to eliminate the short last line, but that's making the layout determine the content, always a bad idea.

You could make some of the type smaller, but that's distracting and ugly. Or you could compress some of the text—change the spacing so that letters are just slightly closer together. That's a little different from justification, which changes spaces between words; compressing text can change spaces between individual letters. That's what I propose here (and do here and in my other publications) … with some restrictions.

Let's look at an example. Consider a slightly modified version of the text used in earlier examples.

Example With a Bad Break

Hardly knowing what she did, she picked up a little bit of stick, and held it out to the puppy: whereupon the puppy jumped into the air off all its feet at once, and with a yelp of delight rushed at the stick, and made believe to worry it then Alice dodged behind a great thistle to keep herself from being run over, and, the moment she appeared at the other side, the puppy made another dart at the stick, and tumbled head over heels in its hurry to get hold: then Alice, thinking it was very like having a game of play with a cart-horse, and expecting every moment to be trampled under its feet, ran round the thistle again: then the puppy begin a series of short charges at the stick, running a very little way forwards each time, and barking hoarsely all the while, till at last it sat down a good way off, panting, with its tongue hanging out of its mouth, and its great eyes half shut. Some vandal added words.

There you have it: A bad break, with "words" sitting all by itself.

Example With Copyfitting

Hardly knowing what she did, she picked up a little bit of stick, and held it out to the puppy: whereupon the puppy jumped into the air off all its feet at once, and with a yelp of delight rushed at the stick, and made believe to worry it then Alice dodged behind a great thistle to keep herself from being run over, and, the moment she appeared at the other side, the puppy made another dart at the stick, and tumbled head over heels in its hurry to get hold: then Alice, thinking it was very like having a game of play with a cart-horse, and expecting every moment to be trampled under its feet, ran round the thistle again: then the puppy begin a series of short charges at the stick, running a very little way forwards each time, and barking hoarsely all the while, till at last it sat down a good way off, panting, with its tongue hanging out of its mouth, and its great eyes half shut. Some vandal added words.

Same text, same character size. Looking at those two paragraphs together, do you see anything different, except for the fact that the second instance is a line shorter?

Condensing the Whole Paragraph

What did I do? I condensed the spacing in the second paragraph by the smallest amount, first selecting the whole paragraph, then right-clicking, choosing **Font**, then the **Advanced** tab, and then clicking the down arrow once on the rightmost box next to **Spacing**—which yields **Condensed** in the left box and **0.1 point** in the right box, as in Figure 6.1.

This change allows Microsoft Word to condense the spaces between characters by up to a tenth of a point in order to reduce the overall space required for text.

In most cases, condensing full paragraphs by 0.1, 0.2, or even 0.3 points won't be noticeable to most readers. Similarly, expanding text by 0.1 to 0.3 points may not be noticeable—as long as you do it for an entire paragraph, not just a line or a sentence.

Consider the following examples, using one line and with left alignment to clarify what's happening: The first group shows regular spacing and the same line condensed 0.1, 0.3, 0.5, and 0.7 points. The second group shows regular spacing and then the same line expanded 0.1, 0.3, 0.5, and 0.7 points.

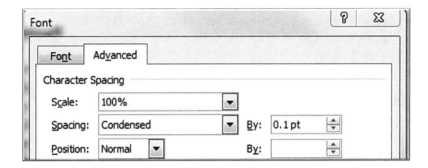

Figure 6.1 Condensing text by 0.1 point

Regular and Condensed Type

An enormous puppy was looking down at her with large eyes.
An enormous puppy was looking down at her with large eyes.
An enormous puppy was looking down at her with large eyes.
An enormous puppy was looking down at her with large eyes.
An enormous puppy was looking down at her with large eyes.

Regular and Expanded Type

An enormous puppy was looking down at her with large eyes.
An enormous puppy was looking down at her with large eyes.
An enormous puppy was looking down at her with large eyes.
An enormous puppy was looking down at her with large eyes.
An enormous puppy was looking down at her with large
eyes.

Character Styles: Making It Faster

I find that copyfitting is much less obvious when applied to an entire
paragraph than when applied to just a line or a sentence. Typography
and layout are supposed to stay out of the way—to keep the reader's
attention on what you've written, not on the type itself. I believe the
tiny change in using slightly condensed or expanded type is essentially
invisible at the paragraph stage, but it's more likely to be noticeable if
it's only used for a sentence or part of a sentence.

Because you'll condense or expand paragraphs slightly to fix bad breaks and to clean up problems with vertical justification, four character styles appear in bk6pv.dotx and bk6pvex.dotx to make this process faster. If you're designing your own template, you might wish to add similar styles—but do so carefully.

Using any of these styles will *undo* italics or boldface type within the paragraph. If you use a lot of italics or bold, you might be better off making changes manually—that is, after selecting a paragraph, right-click, select Font, go to the Advanced tab, and use the up arrow or down arrow on the right-hand box on the Spacing: line to expand or condense the type.

For paragraphs without italics or boldface, styles c1 and c2 condense selected text by 0.1 point or 0.2 point, respectively. Styles e1 and e2 expand selected text by the same amounts. You should *only* use these styles on full paragraphs, following these steps:

1. Triple-click to select the paragraph.
2. Click on c1 or e1 on the style palette or quick list to condense or expand by 0.1 point.
3. If that doesn't do the job, click on c2 or e2. (If you need to condense or expand by 0.3 point, use the manual technique just described—but do this sparingly, as 0.3 point can be visible.)
4. To undo these, triple-click on the paragraph and use Ctrl-Space to undo all character modifications. If you have special characters in the paragraph, you can right-click, go to the Advanced tab on the Font dialog box, and change Spacing back to Normal (or adjust the value to 0, which does the same thing).

Vertical Alignment

Technically, all documents have vertical alignment. What I mean here is *justified* vertical alignment—adding small vertical spaces between paragraphs so the last line of each page is at the exact same place.

Many books don't have justified vertical alignment, but most of the best-designed ones do. Vertical justification is regarded as one sign of a professionally laid out book, at least when it's done right—that is, when it doesn't leave *big* vertical spaces between paragraphs.

Word supports justified vertical alignment, but there's a problem. Word takes it literally, justifying the text on *every* page, including the last page of each chapter or section. The results may be amusing, with enormous gaps between paragraphs in some cases, but they're not really what you want to have.

The fix for the last-page problem is fast and easy (even though it may seem a little odd), but there may be other problems with vertical alignment. Those can be fixed by using the same techniques as copyfitting. Design programs such as QuarkXPress have a range of tools and options to fix spacing issues that aren't available in Word. Copyfitting is Word's primary tool to fix spacing issues but may yield results that you find unsatisfactory. Even if you decide not to use vertical justification, copyfitting will minimize extra white space at the bottom of pages, making your book more polished in appearance.

Turning on Vertical Justification

Here's the easiest way to turn on vertical justification:

➢ Go to the start of the first section where you want justified vertical alignment to be in effect—usually the first actual chapter.

➢ On the **Page Layout** tab, click the little arrow at the bottom right of the **Page Setup** area.

➢ In the resulting **Page Setup** dialog box, select the **Layout** tab.

➢ Change **Vertical alignment** to **Justified**—and change **Apply to** to **This point forward**. The dialog box should look something like Figure 6.2.

➢ Click **OK** to apply.

➢ Now, go to the first section where this should *not* apply—probably the index, but possibly an earlier section of back matter. Do the same thing but change **Vertical alignment** back to **Top**.

That's it—but you'll now see that the last page of each chapter, or at least most chapters, looks awful. It's easy to fix them, but there may also be other pages where the space between paragraphs is too big.

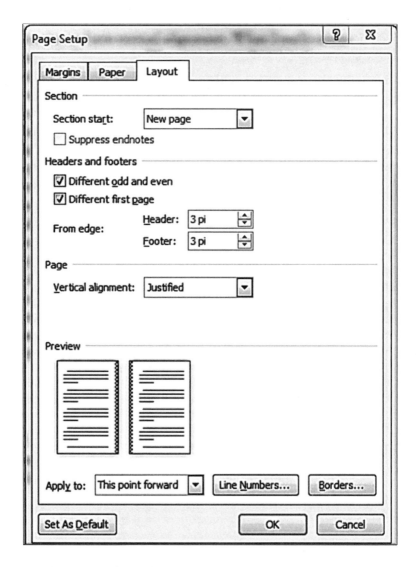

Figure 6.2 Vertical justification

Fixing Awkward Pages

If a page is only one line short, the added space between paragraphs may be barely noticeable. If a page is two lines short—the most it can be unless headings are involved—the added space may be acceptable, if you have several short paragraphs. Any more than that, and the added space is awkward. You're most likely to get really awkward situations just before a heading or subheading, since the heading or subheading *must* be on the same page as the first two lines of the paragraph below it.

You can avoid awkward spacing by copyfitting—expanding or condensing paragraphs to use more or fewer lines. If need be, you can condense or expand paragraphs up to 0.4 point, but try for less if you can. In this book, I never needed to condense or expand paragraphs by more than 0.2 point. On any given page, you should be condensing one or more paragraphs to remove lines or expanding one or more paragraphs to add lines. (In general, I think it makes sense to try removing lines first, but sometimes you really need to add a line or two.)

The fewer headings you have, the less trouble you'll have with awkward spacing. Once in a while, you may find that it's almost impossible to avoid ugly spaces between paragraphs without expanding or condensing so much that it interferes with readability. In that case, you might make an exception, leaving a page short by adding blank paragraphs at the bottom of the page, as in the method for fixing chapter ends described in the next section.

Fixing Chapter Ends

Go to the last page of the first chapter or other section that has justified vertical alignment. (If you have the **Navigation** panel open, this is easy to do—click on the second chapter, then back up one page.)

Go to the end of the last paragraph, which will now be at the bottom of the page. Set the view so you can see the bottom of this page and the start of the next chapter.

Hit Enter.

Keep hitting Enter until you jump to the next page—at which point, Backspace one space to erase that last paragraph mark.

At this point, the last page of the chapter should look right: You've added enough dummy paragraphs (all those Enters) to correct the spacing problem.

Now do the same thing for each chapter. Make sure you delete that last Enter in each case!

That's it. Your book now has even pages. Look at the results. If you like it better without justified vertical alignment, you know what to do: Change vertical alignment back to **Top**.

Too Much Trouble?

Does this process—fixing bad breaks and adjusting pages so that vertical justification looks good—sound like it takes forever? It shouldn't be nearly that bad. Even in a book as thick with subheadings as this one is, the process is surprisingly fast once you start doing it.

It seems to take me 15 minutes to half an hour, at most, to deal with one chapter (fixing bad breaks and adjusting for vertical justification at the same time), and that's adding another variable: a house style that attempts to assure that line-breaking hyphens never leave two letters at the end or beginning of a line.

One word of caution: Don't try to do the entire book in one sitting. Take a break after each chapter. You'll stay fresh and are more likely to do a good job.

Alternative Approaches

LibreOffice supports condensed and expanded type, but the process is significantly more cumbersome. Here's what you have to do:

➢ Select the text.

➢ Right-click and choose **Character.**

➢ Select the **Position** tab.

➢ On the **Spacing** line, first change **Normal** to **Condensed** or **Expanded.**

➢ Then key in **0.1** in the box after "**by**" (or in some cases 0.2 or 0.3 or 0.4).

➢ Click on **OK.**

Two things make this more cumbersome. First, you have to change Normal to Condensed *first*—the by box is grayed out until you do that. Second, and much worse, the up-down arrows change by 1.0 point, an enormous change that will wreck body type. Here's "an enormous change that will wreck body type" condensed by 1.0 point—it's hard to read, to put it mildly.

Realistically, LibreOffice/OpenOffice's Spacing tool is designed for headlines and other cases where visual spacing is important.

I can't find evidence that LibreOffice supports vertical alignment.

7
Front and Back Matter

There's more to a book than the body of the text. This chapter will note most of the elements you *might* have as front and back matter and which of those are nearly mandatory.

Front Matter

The rules for making front matter look good and work well are the same as for the body of the book, with a few exceptions:

➢ Don't use Heading 1 through Heading 3—as is or with modifications—for front sections before the table of contents and typically not for the table of contents itself. Why? Because you'll almost certainly use Microsoft Word's built-in functions to generate your table of contents—and that function relies on Heading 1 through Heading 3. The **Front** style in bk6pv.dotx is the same as Heading 1 but doesn't generate an entry in the table of contents.

➢ Front matter normally has no page numbers before the table of contents and roman numerals from the table of contents through the end of the front matter. The first chapter of the book's body should be page 1 and marks the start of Arabic numbers. Typically, running headers also begin with the table of contents (if it runs to more than one page).

➢ You would typically not use vertical justification for front matter before and including the table of contents.

Title and Copyright Pages

Many books begin with a half title page, consisting of nothing more than the title of the book—sometimes without the subtitle. When used, the back (verso) of the half title page will be blank (unless you have written other books and choose to list them here or wish to include blurbs for your book). Half title pages can be useful as places for authors to autograph books and, in traditional publishing, can work to even out printing signatures and reduce the number of blank pages at the back of the book—but they aren't mandatory. If you wish to save 4 cents per copy and don't see the point, omit the half title page.

The title page is mandatory and is always a recto (right-hand) page. The title page contains up to six elements, from top to bottom, and rarely much more: title, subtitle, edition (if any), author's name, publisher's name, and place of publication.

Frequently, all elements of the title page are centered, with the title having the largest and most prominent type, the subtitle smaller type, the edition statement (if present) smaller still, a gap, the author's name in some intermediate type size, and, near the bottom of the page, the publisher's name (and logo), location, and (if present) year of publication. But none of those norms is written in stone. Two of my professionally published books have my name *above* the title, because they use the cover design as the title page and that's how the covers were designed.

You say you don't have a publisher's name—this is a micropublication and you're not planning to make a career of this sort of thing? Then don't bother: Just put the city, state, and year at the bottom of the page. Come up with a balance of placement, type size, and typeface that looks good. If you've prepared a special design for the title and author name as part of the cover, consider reusing that design on the title page.

The copyright page is also mandatory and (almost) always appears on the verso of the title page. How much you include here depends on what you're doing with your book and what other front matter you have. You'll probably repeat the title at the top of the page. You should have a copyright statement—"Copyright © 2012 by Jane Author" will do, noting that when you key a capital C surrounded by parentheses Word automatically converts it to the copyright symbol (or you can add it using the Symbol list). I don't see much reason to add the usual "All rights reserved …" paragraph for a micropublished book, and note that you *cannot* legally prevent all copying in any case. This page is the best place to add your full contact information if you wish to provide it.

What else goes on the copyright page? If you have an ISBN, it should appear here. If you have cataloging in publication (CIP) data—highly unlikely for a micropublication—it appears on the copyright page. If you need to give credit for the cover design or a photo on the cover, this is a good place to do so. If you have specific credits, you can put them either here or in a separate Acknowledgments page. I've seen copyright pages crammed with text from top to bottom; I've also seen (and produced) pages with only three lines of type. Your micropublication probably won't need loads of wording.

I talk a little more about copyright in a later chapter, but you might consider whether your micropublication is a good candidate for a Creative Commons license, explicitly allowing others to copy all or part of it with certain restrictions. If so, you should determine which license you need, then print the license information on the copyright page.

If you choose to have a colophon—information on how the book was produced—the copyright page is one excellent place for it, although a colophon can also be its own page in either front matter or back matter, with or without *Colophon* as a label. A colophon should, at a minimum, say what typefaces are used in a book; it can additionally mention software used for layout and credit people involved in the production if you've outsourced some steps.

Other Pre-Contents Pages

Do you want to dedicate your book to someone? A great way to do that is with a dedication page, typically the next (right-hand) page after the copyright page. A good dedication page might have nothing more than a single line of type or paragraph saying something like "To x" and why the book's being dedicated to x. You don't need "Dedication" as a heading. Keep it simple, keep it clean. The verso of the dedication page—if you have one—will be blank in most cases.

You might also have an epigraph, a short quote or poem that seems important to the book. If you want an epigraph page, it works like the dedication page: very simple, on a recto page, with the verso blank.

Contents Page

It's a rare book (at least where nonfiction is concerned) that has no table of contents—and if you've used Heading 1 and Heading 2 consistently, it's a snap to create and maintain your table of contents.

Just start a new section or at least a new right-hand page, provide an appropriate heading (e.g., Contents or Table of Contents), then—where you'd start inserting text after that heading—open the **References** tab, click on **Table of Contents** at the far left, and click on **Insert Table of Contents**. In the dialog box, choose the number of levels to include in the table of contents—the default is 3, but you may want to change that to 2 or even 1 to avoid a very long table of contents—and click **OK**.

There it is: your table of contents, using built-in styles TOC 1, TOC 2, and TOC 3 (if you include three levels of heading). You may need to modify those styles—for example, TOC 1 may be indented because it's based on Normal—but they work pretty well. As with most built-in styles, these won't show up in the styles palette until they're used, and maybe not then. If that's the case, click on **Options** in the styles palette and change **Select styles to show** to **All** long enough to make the modifications. Alternatively, you could take one of the proffered designs that include text for the heading as well as styles for the contents.

You can generate your table of contents as soon as you have at least one heading and go back later, after you've done all the editing, right-click anywhere within the table of contents, and choose **Update field** to refresh the actual table of contents.

It's possible to modify the table of contents directly, but try to avoid that if you can. The process is clumsy, and the next time you make changes that add or subtract pages, you'll have to refresh the table of contents anyway, wiping out your modifications.

How many levels of content should you show? That's up to you and depends on your book. The tables of contents in most of my books have only included chapters, but it's not at all uncommon to include main headings and subheadings (two levels) as in this book—and I've seen books that usefully included three levels. If you're doing a family history arranged by decade with major topics within each decade, two levels would seem natural.

Sections after the table of contents should use Heading 1 for section names, since those sections should appear in the table of contents. However, sections after the table of contents still use roman page numbers—up to the body of the book.

Foreword

A foreword is written by somebody else—that is, someone other than the author. It may be an essay by a person who has a big name in the area you are writing about or a fellow author in your genre endorsing your work.

If you're publishing the reminiscences of an ancestor, you may write the foreword yourself. Forewords are entirely optional. Do note the spelling—it's foreword, not forward!

Preface

How did this book come about? If there's an interesting story to tell, the preface is a good place to tell it. The editor of a teen poetry anthology might use a preface to discuss the poetry group and the selection process; you might tell the story of how you gathered your family's stories. Prefaces can be much more informal and personal than the rest of a book. It's not unusual to include brief acknowledgments in the preface and skip the following section. A preface is usually short, typically no more than two or three pages. Otherwise, the content might better be treated as an introduction.

Acknowledgments

If you have a bunch of people to thank for helping make the book possible or granting permission to use quotations or photographs, you probably need an Acknowledgments section. It shouldn't go on too long (Jennifer Basye Sanders suggests that if you need more than three pages for acknowledgments, you should move the section to appear just before the index). You can equally well acknowledge people in your preface or introduction.

Introduction

This is likely to be the last section of the front matter—and with luck your book won't need all of these sections! Where a preface may be about how the book came to be, the introduction is about the book itself—what it's about and how it's structured. Of course, an introduction can also *be* a preface that's more than three pages long.

Special Cases

Some books benefit from other sections of front matter. For example, this book has an About the Website page in the front matter.

Back Matter

After the last chapter of your book come appendices and other back matter—all of which are optional, all of which continue with Arabic numbering, and all of which should use Heading 1 as section titles. Think of these as chapters that don't have chapter numbers. There's no absolute set order to back matter, except that the afterword (if any) usually comes first and the index usually comes last.

Afterword

If you feel the need to wrap things up in a manner that doesn't fit in your final chapter, here's your chance. There's not much more to say.

Appendices

You may have one or more appendices: lists, resources, stuff that's needed to flesh out the book and that doesn't fit into the book itself. You may choose to label each appendix as Appendix A: name of appendix, Appendix B: name of appendix, and so on.

Endnotes and Footnotes

Where do you put notes? There are three possible places, all more-or-less directly supported by Word:

1. As footnotes at the bottom of each page
2. As endnotes at the end of each chapter (or, really, section)
3. As endnotes at the end of the book

If you choose #3 and have more than a handful of notes, you'll probably want to put all of the endnotes in their own section, probably labeled Notes.

You can mix #1 and either #2 or #3, offering substantive footnotes at the bottom of pages and source endnotes (citations) at the end of each chapter or the whole book. If you do that, you should use separate numbering schemes for endnotes and footnotes. Word can be tricky about formatting footnotes, including adding more space above the footnote separator than may seem reasonable and doing other things you may find difficult or impossible to correct. There's a built-in Footnote style you can modify, used for both footnotes and endnotes.

Glossary

Do you need a glossary? Quite possibly not for many family histories and similar books, but you may find one useful. A glossary should clarify special terms that appear in your book, particularly ones where your usage is unusual. A glossary can also include other terms related to the book's topic, even if they don't appear in the text. Most glossaries are alphabetic, unless there's a reason to have subglossaries separated by headings. Each glossary entry usually consists of a single paragraph beginning with the term and a colon (both in bold) followed by the definition.

I've provided the **bibgloss** style in bk6pv.dotx as a typical way to handle regular entries in this and the next section. It uses a hanging indent for the first line and adds 6 points blank space above and below (or between) each entry.

Bibliography

The **bibgloss** style should also work for bibliography entries, which should be done using a consistent citation style and may or may not include annotations or discussions of some or all books and other sources. (If your entries are annotated, you may prefer the **bib** style, used in this book, which adds 12 points space above each entry, twice as much space as **bibgloss**.)

Your bibliography may not be called a bibliography. If you leave out some minor references, it should be called what it is: A Selected Bibliography. If it's a list that includes not only what you read to write the book but also other things you recommend to the reader, it's probably Recommended Reading. There are other possibilities—and you could have more than one section of bibliography or more than one alphabetic list with subheadings. You'll note that this book's bibliography includes a paragraph of commentary after some citations; I didn't call it an Annotated Bibliography, but that's what it is.

About the Author

This is the one piece of back matter that *could* reasonably appear after the index, but I'd include it just before—if you feel it's needed and haven't already covered this ground. This page (and it's usually no more than a page) is written in the third person: It may be *by* you but it's *about* you.

Index

There are many ways to produce a good index—and probably no part of a nonfiction book (other than the cover) that can benefit more from the work of an expert. I'm not an expert indexer and am unqualified to tell you how to prepare an excellent index, or even what should be included (other than the obvious: names of people and significant topics).

You can't generate an index until all your other editing and copyfitting is complete: This is just about the last thing you do in a book before uploading it.

There are effectively three ways to get an index into your book when you're using Word to do the production:

1. Tag index entries within Word and let it do the work.
2. Create a dummy Word document consisting entirely of index entries, then import the generated index into your book.
3. Do the whole thing manually, then use suitable Index styles to tag the index you've created.

I'll discuss them in reverse order.

Manual Indexing

Many of you will, quite appropriately, use the third technique. You'll use index cards or whatever to note places where a topic needs to be indexed or a significant name appears, alphabetize all of those items, then prepare an index. You can start the new section with Index as Heading 1, then tag most index entries as Index 1, subentries as Index 2, and so on. If you want a two-column index, you'll need to start a new section (continuous) immediately after the Index heading, then change the Page Layout to two columns from that point forward.

Or you can let Word do part of the work.

The Dummy Document Approach

In this case, you start another blank document, typing each item on page one that needs an index entry, just as you'd want it in the index. Then start a new page (Ctrl-Enter is one fast way) and add items on page two, and continue until you're done. You'll probably want to keep this document in draft view (the rightmost option on the bottom bar, just left of the zoom percentage) so it's not too jumpy.

Now—or as you finish each page—highlight each entry, use **Alt-Shift-X** (or **Mark Entry** on the **References** tab) to mark the text as an index item, and continue until you're done. (There may be a way to automate this process, but if so I haven't found it.)

Then start a new section and click on **Insert Index** in the **References** tab. You can now copy that text—the index for your dummy book—to the Index section of your actual book.

This sounds clumsy. It *is* clumsy. The advantage is that you can't possibly screw up your actual book in the process. (I use this process to index my ejournal, *Cites & Insights*, but that's partly because one index covers multiple issues and I can use chapters to simulate issues.)

Note that you can, along the way, add *See* and *See Also* references and build a two-level index.

Indexing Within Word

You can also mark text as index entries within your book, then use **Insert Index** to prepare your index. That's probably the most natural way to do it, but it requires a few caveats:

➢ Remember that names need to be reversed for the index—that is, if you mark "Jane Grandmere" in the text, you'll need to change the **Main Entry** to "Grandmere, Jane" in the **Mark Index Entry** dialog box.

➢ Be very cautious when using **Mark All**! This sounds like a real winner—you encounter the first appearance of John Grandpere, change the **Main Entry**, and now you can index all the appearances with just one stroke. And so you can ... but you can also completely wreck your book! That's most likely to happen because you use **Mark All** on text that appears within a running header or footer—and the results are calamitous. (Remember: If you're indexing a word, that string of letters may also appear within a longer word.) If you're absolutely certain this won't happen, then **Mark All** is a time-saver ... but I'd suggest saving a separate copy of the book under a different name before you try it out.

➤   The other warning on **Mark All** is to use "shorter may appear within longer" caution. If Jane Grandmere and Jane Grandmere Parsons both appear in your book and you **Mark All** on the first Jane Grandmere … well, you can guess what happens.

➤   Word doesn't do a great job of marking page ranges for indexed items, it limits an index to two levels (main entries and subentries), and it doesn't highlight the most important page numbers. You can modify the index once it's produced to take care of this.

➤   You probably already know that a good index notes concepts, not just words—it uses the same term for the same concept throughout, even when that concept is discussed using different terms. An index is not a concordance: You should be noting where topics are discussed, not just where specific words appear.

That's It

Your book is complete—other than a cover, that is. You've proofread everything. You know that all sections are in the right order. You've done your copyfitting and other grunt work. The pages look right on the screen and on your test printout.

Take a break. Celebrate. Continue with the remaining steps to seeing your book as a book: the cover, PDF issues, and dealing with your provider.

8
Cover, Copyright, and Other Matters

Every book needs a cover—and the skills required to make great covers are not the same as those required to write great books. If you have friends, family members, or colleagues of a more artistic bent, this may be the time to get them involved.

This chapter deals with ways to create a cover but also with a few other matters you should consider before completing your book, such as whether you need an ISBN, copyright issues, and possibly paying others to handle some steps in micropublishing.

Creating a Cover

Both micropublishing service providers—Lulu and CreateSpace—offer several ways to create a cover, and there's a fair amount of similarity between the two. You have six choices:

➢ *Text Only*: Use the provider's cover wizard to choose a cover template that's type-only or includes some predesigned figures.

➢ *Cover With Pictures*: Similar to Text Only, but using a template with places reserved to insert pictures, which you upload. This may be the most common route for straightforward micropublications.

➢ *Cover Template With Downloading and Modification*: You start with a cover template but download the results and edit them on your own computer. (This may not always be possible in CreateSpace.)

➢ *Do-It-Yourself, Front Cover and Back Cover Only*: You replace the entire front (and optionally back) of a cover wizard template with a cover you've prepared at home.

➢ *Do-It-Yourself One-Piece*: You prepare the entire cover—front, spine, and back—on your computer, uploading it as a single file.

➢ *Paid Cover Design*: You pay someone else to design your cover, either using your service provider as an intermediary (for $300 and up) or hiring your own cover designer.

The last option undermines the low-cost/no-cost theme of this book—are you going to pay $300 to have a cover designed for a book that will only see ten to fifty copies produced? I mention it as a possibility but won't write more about it. A few notes on other options follow.

Most of my own Lulu books use Do-It-Yourself One-Piece covers, but one uses what's effectively a Text Only cover. My wife uses the Cover With Pictures option for her family histories, using portraits and creating photomontages suitable to the family.

If you spend time in the community forums on Lulu, you'll frequently see suggestions such as "then download it and use Photoshop to fix it up." Unless you already own Photoshop, that's *not* a low-cost/no-cost option. My wife has used the low-cost Corel Paint Shop Pro to create and modify photomontages and add cover type. I've been reasonably happy using the no-cost Paint.NET to clean up photos and add cover text.

You can start thinking about cover design any time, but you generally can't finish the job until the body of your book is complete or very nearly so. For some cover options, it's impossible to complete a cover design until you know the book's final page count, and the publishing process at Lulu and CreateSpace assumes you'll be done with the body of the book before you work on the cover.

Still, you *can* do much of the work in parallel—deciding what you want in a cover and finding certain resources.

What Do You Want?

Your cover should enhance your book and be consonant with the book. That's a given. You probably wouldn't use a cover full of playful clip art images, with the title and author in Comic Sans or Bradley Hand, for a book offering the story of how your forebears came to

California—unless, I suppose, they ventured across the country as part of a traveling circus.

But covers allow enormous leeway. Sometimes, a direct relationship between the cover design and the book contents seems obvious and works beautifully. For example, you could use a great sepia picture of your great-great grandparents (or a collage of family forebears) as the primary cover element in a book on the history of that part of your family, or a picture of a local park in a book detailing trails and activities in local parks.

Other times, the cover can be purely abstract—an abstract design (you'll find some of these in templates) and the usual cover text or, possibly, just text on a color background.

The cover might bear a design that's not directly related to the book's content but doesn't fight with that content. That's what I've done in several self-published books, using travel photos that seemed particularly nice but had no direct contextual significance.

What do you want? One photo on each cover (front and back)? A collage on one or both covers? Original artwork or something scanned from source material? Did that pioneer include drawings in his diary or her journal?

You don't need to worry about the *inside* front or back cover: Neither Lulu nor CreateSpace allows for anything to be printed on that side: It's always blank.

Can You Use That Picture?

Pictures—either photographs or artwork—make great book covers, but you may not have the rights to use a particular picture.

A photo handed down in the family that you know was taken by a family member? Unless another family member objects, you probably have use rights.

A photo of family members taken by a commercial photographer more recently than 1923? Oddly enough, you might *not* have the right to use that photo—at least not if you're planning to sell copies of the book. (That's true whether it's on the cover or within the book.) That may seem stupid and it may *be* stupid, but it's the law.

A photo from a magazine or a picture that you love? You almost certainly do *not* have the right to use it without contacting the copyright owner for permission (and probably payment). If you use such a photo anyway, you'll be perjuring yourself when you upload the book, since both Lulu and CreateSpace require that you certify that you have the right to use any materials in your uploads. You're also risking an enormous fine for copyright infringement; it's just not worth the risk.

There are sources of free photos that explicitly allow you to use them, including high-definition photos that would work well for book covers. A little searching on the internet should yield good possibilities. Be careful: Some such sources allow any *non-commercial* use, which does not include a book that's for sale.

A photo that *you* took of your family or of some natural scene, or of artwork you created? That's *your* photograph. You own the copyright, and you have full rights to use it.

Let's step through each of the five potentially cost-free means of preparing a cover.

Text Only Cover

This can be dead simple. The cover wizard at your provider will offer a variety of cover design possibilities, each of which will include your title, subtitle, and author byline, and also the title and author byline on the spine (if the book is thick enough). Lulu's new Cover Wizard, for example, offers a choice of background color, several choices for layout, and a number of themes, which can even include graphic designs, although they'll be designs used on other Lulu books.

You should be able to choose one of a number of typefaces, although the choices will probably be narrower than those for your book. You should be able to decide how large you want each text element to be. You may have the option of adding text, such as a descriptive paragraph or two (or blurbs) on the back cover.

You can probably select whatever color you'd like for the background and an appropriately contrasting color for the type. You'll be offered a range of colors but should also have the option of specifying an absolute color value in hexadecimal notation, which you can typically figure out using almost any graphics program—or, for that matter, use an eyedropper in a graphics program (or in the cover wizard) to select a color from an image you've uploaded for the cover.

Some Lulu cover themes are quite attractive, and some include spots to add your own photograph or back cover text. If you don't want to spend much time making a cover, these might be appropriate.

Cover With Pictures

Some canned layouts and themes include spots for one or more photographs. You may also be able to overlay photos in other layouts and themes. The main things to remember when adding pictures (either photos or other images) to covers are:

➢ Make sure you have the right to use the pictures.

➢ Make sure the pictures are saved at 300 dpi or higher. Lower-resolution pictures won't look good. If you're submitting a JPEG, use a high-quality version; don't try to save space here.

➢ Make sure the size is right.

➢ Just because the cover is printed in full color doesn't mean you must use full-color photos. Sometimes, a black-and-white (grayscale) or sepia photo is more effective than a full-color photo.

In my experience, cover photos that are uploaded at 300 dpi usually come out looking great, but you do need to allow for some variation in color. When I've done the same book through both CreateSpace and Lulu, literally using the same cover in both cases, the resulting covers haven't been absolutely identical, but they've been within an acceptable range.

Cover Template With Downloading and Modification

Let's say you start with a cover template but find you want to tweak it more than the cover wizard allows. In many, probably most, cases— certainly for Lulu—you can download the cover, modify it in a graphics program, and upload it again.

If you plan to modify text on the cover, delete the text that's already there before downloading the cover. Otherwise, you'll find it almost impossible to deal with, since text will be downloaded as pixels, not as type. It's easier to modify images than it is to modify text.

Do-It-Yourself Front (and Back) Cover

This option gives you more control but also more responsibility. You'll be uploading a graphic as the entire front cover and, optionally, another as the entire back cover. The provider (Lulu or CreateSpace) provides spine type, but it's up to you to make sure the color of the spine is consistent with (and preferably identical to) the color background for front and back covers.

If you're doing this, you've looked at enough covers to have a feel for relative type sizes and placement for the book title, subtitle, author name(s), and, if used, publisher name. You know what graphics you want to use and that you have the rights to use those images.

Two more issues come into play: cover size and flow.

Cover Size

The front cover image for a 6" x 9" book is *not* 6 inches by 9 inches (or 1,800 x 2,700 pixels, if you're preparing a graphics file). You have to allow for a *bleed* on all outer sides—that is, an extra 0.125" (37.5 pixels) above, below, and to the outside of the cover. A front cover would actually be 1,838 pixels wide and 2,775 pixels high.

It's never safe to put anything significant, such as type, within 0.125" of the edge of the page—that's the variance allowed for printing and binding irregularities. That means there should never be text or significant image details within the 38 pixels (0.125") nearest any edge of the image. Realistically, margins for type should be much wider than that, say at least half an inch on either side and an inch top and bottom.

Flow

The placement of the spine may also be off by up to 0.125". That means you should never use vertical lines to differentiate among the front cover, spine, and back cover, and you should always use the same background color for all three portions.

Do-It-Yourself One-Piece

I *love* one-piece book covers, but they may not suit your needs. For several of my books, I've taken a photo I particularly like—either a digital photo or a very high-resolution scan of a print photo— trimmed it to the exact size of the cover, touched it up as needed, and added cover and spine text to the photo.

There are three issues to consider if you're doing something like this, apart from whether it's the look you want for a book and whether you have rights for the photo:

➤ You can't create a do-it-yourself one-piece cover until you know precisely how thick the spine will be, and you won't know that until you've finished working on the interior of the book and you have a final page count. At that point, Lulu and CreateSpace offer calculators to show exactly how large the cover should be (in inches and in pixels at 300 pixels per inch). The calculator includes required bleed space.

➤ Really big pictures show flaws. How big is really big? The cover for *Cites & Insights 9: 2009*—the largest volume of that ejournal, with 434 8.5" x 11" pages—is 5,468 pixels wide by 3,375 pixels high—in other words, 18.23" x 11.25". (The spine is just under an inch thick.) That's a *big* picture. A micropublished book can run to more than 700 pages, requiring an even bigger picture.

➤ Depending on the graphics editor you use, you may find setting the spine type a little difficult. In Paint.NET, for example, your best bet is to add a new transparent layer, type in what you need, then rotate that layer 90 degrees, and adjust it until it's in the right place. In some programs, type is an independent element until you're done with it, rotatable in its own right. (You always need to combine all layers into a single flat layer before saving a cover for uploading.)

If you go this route, you might find it useful to add a dummy layer with vertical lines at both edges of the spine and a line centered in the actual front cover (excluding bleed), to make it easier to put type in the right place. You might even add horizontal lines to guide your type. Make sure to delete that dummy layer before finishing the cover.

Take Your Time

The cover matters—not so much as a marketing device for a micropublished book, but as the first impression a reader has of a book. Take your time. You may need to try several possibilities. For that matter, you may find that you're unhappy with the cover when you receive your first copy of the book. That's OK: You can replace the cover before you make the book available for others to buy.

You can't get too fancy. Embossed type, metallic foil, cutouts—none of these are feasible for micropublished books. But you can do a lot with good full-color printing and thoughtful design.

ISBN

Until recently, your choice on whether to have an ISBN on your micropublication was straightforward. If you used CreateSpace, you had one—automatically. If you used Lulu, adding an ISBN was an extra-cost option, one you probably wouldn't choose for a true micropublication.

That's changed: Lulu will now provide an ISBN for free. Does that mean you should always take one? Not necessarily.

If you believe your book can be sold in bookstores, you want an ISBN. If you want your book to be in *Books in Print*, you *need* an ISBN—but having an ISBN does not automatically get you into *Books in Print*. For some online sales channels, an ISBN may be important. Otherwise, it's not clear that an ISBN offers any real advantage.

Implications of a Lulu or CreateSpace ISBN

If you accept a Lulu or CreateSpace ISBN—as opposed to *not* requesting a Lulu ISBN or having your own ISBN for CreateSpace (improbable for a micropublisher)—Lulu or CreateSpace becomes the publisher of record.

That means Lulu or CreateSpace will be listed as the publisher in any bibliographic feeds. It means you can't use that ISBN if you choose to republish the book with a different publisher. For Lulu, it also means that your payments become royalties (and will be reported to the IRS, so you'll have to file a W9 form with Lulu).

Note that each edition of a book has its own ISBN. So, for example, if you change the book's title, binding, or size, you need a new ISBN. If you change the book's text substantially enough to call it a new edition, you also need a new ISBN.

Should You Use an ISBN?

You should absolutely use an ISBN if you plan to sell the book through channels other than Lulu—although Amazon does sell some Lulu books that don't have ISBNs. Since CreateSpace insists on an ISBN for every book, it's not a question with CreateSpace.

I haven't bothered with ISBNs for most of my micropublished books in the past, except for CreateSpace versions. I've seen the claim that (some) libraries are actively hostile to Lulu and CreateSpace ISBNs—that they regard them as a sign of inferior books. But I've also seen the claim that (some) libraries won't buy books that don't have ISBNs. I'm sure both claims are true for some libraries, and I have no idea what "some" means in either case.

Copyright and Creative Commons

Your book is protected by copyright. That's true in every case. The text in your book is protected by copyright as soon as you print it out and, perhaps, as soon as you save it to disk. Not only is your book protected by copyright, that protection lasts until you've been dead for 70 years — assuming the term isn't extended further.

That does *not* mean you can play the copyright violation lottery, that game where you hope to hit somebody with a $250,000 fine for infringing on your copyright. To play the copyright violation lottery, you need to *register* your copyrighted items — and you need to do so within three months of publication.

Technically, you're required to submit two copies of the "best edition" of your book to the Library of Congress (LC) *if the book is available for public sale*. Submitting those two copies does not ensure that LC will retain your book. If you fail to do so — and many micropublishers do — LC can demand copies. At that point, you would most definitely send LC the two copies. Registration adds a fee of $35 (electronic submission) to $65 (paper submission), most typically paid along with the deposit copies. Do you need to do this for micropublications? Only if you're really worried about copyright infringement.

You can't sue somebody for copyright infringement until you've registered the copyright — and you can't sue them for *statutory* damages (the huge sums you see mentioned on DVDs and elsewhere) unless you've registered copyright within three months of publication. Otherwise, the most you can sue for is actual damages.

As a matter of course, you'll probably insert a copyright notice on your back-of-title page. Should you register your copyright? Are you worried about copyright infringement? Before you decide, consider the Creative Commons alternative.

Adding a Creative Commons License

What's the purpose of your micropublication? For many authors, it will be to record your family's stories — or your own stories — for the benefit of your family and descendants, as well as your relatives. There are many other purposes for very short-run books. For most micropublishers, the primary purpose is not to make money, or at least it shouldn't be: The economics of micropublishing don't work in your favor.

If you're passing along family history, you should hope that somebody else down the road will take what you've done and add to it, forming a richer story. By the time they do that, you may be hard to contact. You can help them by adding a Creative Commons (CC) license to your work.

Creative Commons (creativecommons.org) is "a nonprofit organization that develops, supports, and stewards legal and technical infrastructure that maximizes digital creativity, sharing, and innovation." More specifically, Creative Commons crafts legal methods to grant additional rights to reuse copyrighted material, over and above those already present in fair use, first sale, and other rights.

With one exception—CC0, the assertion that a work is in the public domain—Creative Commons licenses don't negate or conflict with copyright. Instead, they enhance copyright by making a work more useful.

For many of us, the Creative Commons Attribution (CC-BY) license may be ideal. Here's the formal description:

> This license lets others distribute, remix, tweak, and build upon your work, even commercially, as long as they credit you for the original creation. This is the most accommodating of licenses offered. Recommended for maximum dissemination and use of licensed materials.

With a CC-BY license on your book—explicitly stated on the back-of-title page, right below the copyright notice, preferably with an appropriate icon as well—your descendants and other family members can take what you've written, add to it, and reuse it, as long as they credit you for your work.

There are other more restrictive CC licenses (such as one that allows people to pass along your work for free but not to make changes to it). One very popular one is CC BY-NC, attribution and non-commercial:

> This license lets others remix, tweak, and build upon your work non-commercially, and although their new works must also acknowledge you and be non-commercial, they don't have to license their derivative works on the same terms.

The problem with CC BY-NC is that "non-commercial" is a tricky term. If a nephew decides to combine your family history with the next generation's history in a new micropublication sold *primarily* to others in the family, is that non-commercial? According to some, "sold" makes it commercial.

Hundreds of millions of things—ebooks, music, video clips, photographs—already carry Creative Commons licenses. (The CC website includes a long list of content sources with counts for each one. The largest is probably Flickr, with more than 197 million CC-licensed photos as of October 2011.) You'll be in good company with a CC license, and your work will be more useful to others. If you are using a CC license, I wouldn't bother registering your micropublication with the copyright office: It's unlikely you'll be suing anyone for copyright infringement.

Outsourcing

You can pay to outsource almost every step in micropublishing, up to and including the writing itself. Lulu and CreateSpace offer packages to handle various pieces, and there are many other sources to take over some chores.

You need to think carefully about outsourcing, particularly for editorial chores. While good copyediting may be worth paying for if you don't trust your own editing and can't find someone to help you with it, some editorial outsourcing may promise more than it delivers. As soon as you start paying for publishing steps, you move *very* rapidly away from the low-cost/no-cost model: Fees will start in the hundreds and move rapidly to thousands of dollars.

Outsourcing for Free

You need other eyes to look at your manuscript, at least for some level of editing and, ideally, proofreading. It's hard for even the best writers and editors to edit their own copy, much less proofread something they've been working on for so long.

Your friends and family can help, and should be one source of reaction. But you may have other resources.

Does your library have a writers' group you can join? Can you start one? If so, can you swap editorial chores with others in the group?

Your library may be the first and best place not only to learn more about editing and other tasks but also to find others who might be able to help.

Are there other community groups where you could trade outsourcing? I use the word "trade" advisedly: If you're asking someone else to go through your book with a careful eye and red pen (or the electronic equivalent), you should be willing to provide help with some aspect of that writer's work. Bartering editorial services makes sense; freeloading doesn't.

Outsourcing Editing

Should you pay a freelancer to review your manuscript and suggest editorial improvements—traditionally the role of an editor at a publishing house? There are certainly sources happy to do so, and these have existed since long before micropublishing became practical.

In *How to Get Happily Published* (HarperPerennial, 1992), Judith Appelbaum notes the many "criticism services" that advertise in writers' magazines and elsewhere and urges authors to consider the risks of such services:

> Chief among the dangers, perhaps, is the possibility that your whole approach to writing will suffer if you heed the advice of agency critics. For what they're selling is not continuing advice on improving a work in progress but, rather, a one-shot assessment of an allegedly finished manuscript couched primarily in terms of its salability.

This criticism does not apply to writers' workshops, writing groups, and courses on writing, all of which can be useful in improving your writing and your book. It specifically applies to outsourced editorial or manuscript review and revision.

Costs

Consider costs for some of the steps in publishing, using CreateSpace and Lulu service offerings as well as independent quotations. Here are some typical prices for a 60,000-word book:

➢ An editorial evaluation starts at $200, but full-scale editing can cost $800 to $2,700 or more.

➢ Copyediting will run $1,000 to $1,200 for a medium-length manuscript. That should include proofreading.

➢ Interior layout—getting a more interesting template—will run $250 to $700, but processing a Microsoft Word document through a high-end layout program is likely to run $800 to $1,200 or more.

➢ Indexing by a qualified supplier will probably cost $570 to $1,000 or more.

➢ Cover designs can cost as little as $300 for simple options and as much as $1,500 for custom designs with illustrations.

➢ Marketing and distribution will cost a *lot*—starting with $500 or so for a press release with distribution and running $9,500 or more for full-scale marketing campaigns.

If those numbers don't give you pause, you're not a micropublisher. Given the rest of the money you'll spend, buying a high-end layout program and learning to use it, or contracting with a professional to do your typography, is a relatively minor piece, namely $800 to $1,200 to have someone else do it, or $700 (plus learning curve) for the software.

This book is all about doing it on the cheap without the results looking cheap. You need to find people to help, and you need to help them in return, but the template and advice in this book will, I believe, yield a micropublished book that looks as good as most books from large publishers.

9
PDFs and Providers

You've written the book. It's edited, copyedited, proofread, and copyfitted. The front matter's in place, as is the back matter. If there's an index, it's done as well. You've got the cover design.

Now you need to get the project ready to upload—and, if you have not already done so, establish an account with your provider of choice. Then you need to work with that provider's website to turn your project into an actual book.

Service provider websites change. The steps shown in this chapter may look and act differently when you prepare a book. I offer more detail on Lulu because that's the provider I've used most often, but CreateSpace also works (as well in most respects, better in some, not as well in others). For a true micropublication, either one is fine. If you're expanding beyond a small group of readers, you may want to use both. If your project works right on one, it should work right on the other—with certain crucial exceptions, noted later.

PDF Tips and Warnings

If you have Adobe Acrobat already and it plays nicely with Microsoft Word on your system, then you should use it to create your PDFs. Thanks to Distiller, it may produce smaller files than other options noted here. How much smaller? The example used in this chapter, a 209-page 6" x 9" all-text book, is a 4.9 MB file as created directly by Word 2010—and a 1.05 MB file as created through Adobe Acrobat 9 Standard, set to include all typefaces. That's a sizable difference. Additionally, while Lulu can use a PDF created by Word, Lulu says that, should you wish to distribute to other channels, a PDF using Adobe Distiller—that is, one created with Adobe Acrobat—is required.

The key tip for a text only book: You must make sure *all* typefaces are embedded, which involves altering some Adobe Acrobat settings. By default, some standard typefaces such as Arial will not be embedded, and it's likely that your Word file will contain some Arial even though you don't believe you've used any. (I'm not sure whether this is a bug in Word or not, but Adobe Reader consistently shows that there's Arial in every document I create—even though Word's Advanced Find says that there isn't.)

Neither Lulu nor CreateSpace will accept a PDF that does not have all typefaces embedded—noting that they can and should be embedded as partial subsets in most cases.

You must also make sure that Word has paper size (in the **Page Setup** dialog box) set to the book size you're using. Adobe Acrobat and Word's own PDF generator will both respect this setting, which is essential to getting your book produced properly.

If your family history book includes family group sheets or other separate PDFs, you *will* need some program such as Adobe Acrobat that can combine multiple PDFs into a single file—and you may need to use that program's print-to-PDF function, rather than a straight combination, if those PDFs aren't exactly the same page size as the book should be. (Chances are, Adobe Acrobat and other programs will let you mix different page sizes in a single PDF, but Lulu and Create-Space won't accept the resulting file.)

The No-Cost Alternative

You *can* use Word's own PDF function—as long as you make sure one particular setting is on, namely PDF/A. This produces a larger file than the default option (and a much larger file than Adobe Acrobat with Distiller), but it also embeds all typefaces automatically.

To do this, click the **Save & Send** tab on the **File** homepage; click **Create PDF/XPS Document** on the **Save & Send** page; click **Create PDF/XPS** again on the resulting page (in the right column). This will bring up a file dialog box prompting for a filename and location for the PDF—but also a couple of options and, critically, the **Options** button.

Click on **Options**, bringing up the dialog box, the bottom portion of which is shown in Figure 9.1. Then check the **ISO-19005-1 compliant (PDF/A)** option (or make sure it's checked—by default it will *not*

Figure 9.1 PDF/A setting in Create PDF/XPS options

be checked). Then click **OK**. On the file dialog box, make sure **Standard** is checked. Now you can provide a filename and click **Publish**.

There are third-party PDF creators in the $50 range, and there may be free options. To the best of my knowledge, none of them creates files as small as Adobe Acrobat's Distiller, but they should be able to embed all typefaces properly. LibreOffice and OpenOffice have the same PDF/A functionality as Word.

You should double-check your PDF output with Adobe Reader, which is free software. After viewing the pages to make sure it looks the way it should, click **File**, then **Properties**, then **Fonts** in the **Properties** dialog box. Go through the set of typefaces to make sure each one shows "embedded" or "embedded subset." If not, that means you failed to choose PDF/A or, if using Adobe Acrobat, failed to make sure all typefaces are embedded by removing all those that aren't.

This is also the best time to make sure the book looks the way you want it to—and print it out if you're at all unsure. One note on printing a sample copy from Acrobat, as opposed to printing from Word: You may run into trouble if you're printing on both sides of the paper. Since the paper in your printer is probably 8.5" x 11" and you're printing 6" x 9" pages, automatic duplexing may not work— and if you use manual duplexing (where you print all odd-numbered pages, put the stack of pages, flipped over, back in the printer, then print even-numbered pages), your even-numbered pages may not have proper typefaces. This is a quirk or bug in the way Adobe Reader communicates with your printer. I don't know of a workaround.

Putting the Project Together

The book looks the way it should, and you have a complete PDF for the body. You've created a cover (or set of covers) or have an idea how you're going to do that.

Make sure you have all your pieces. You should know your final title and subtitle (and which is which), the exact name of the author, what imprint (publisher) name you're planning to use, and that you have appropriate rights to use any photos or lengthy quoted material.

Now it's time to work with your service provider—and to *choose* a provider if you haven't already done so.

Lulu vs. CreateSpace

Which provider should you use? Lulu or CreateSpace?

You'll find many opinions and write-ups on the choice. That's hardly surprising: These two are the only print on demand service providers that you can use for mostly text books with no up-front costs.

I don't have an easy answer. I've used both (for the same books), but primarily I use Lulu. I've found Lulu easier to work with and generally faster, and at one point I thought Lulu covers were a little truer to the original than the CreateSpace covers. At the same time, under some conditions, CreateSpace is unquestionably cheaper.

If you're reading various online comparisons, it's important to note one cost issue that most of them get wrong. To wit, most say that both Lulu and CreateSpace charge 20 percent when you offer books for sale to others. That's not quite right, and it's a significant issue.

The 20 Percent Issue

For books sold via Lulu, you pay Lulu the production charge plus 20 percent of the *difference* between that charge and the retail price that you set. (Incidentally, when Lulu offers percent-off coupons, which it frequently does, the discount comes out of Lulu's share, not yours.)

For books sold via CreateSpace itself, you pay CreateSpace the production charge plus 20 percent *of the retail price*, including the production charge. Since CreateSpace is part of Amazon, nearly all CreateSpace books wind up on Amazon—and for Amazon, the charge is production price plus *40 percent* of the retail price.

On the other hand, in most cases Lulu's production charge is significantly higher than CreateSpace (the exception being 5.5" x 8.5" "digest-size" books printed on 50# white paper rather than 60# cream paper—we'll get to that in a minute).

Let's say you have a 250-page 6" x 9" paperback that you're certain buyers will pay $35 for (you know your microniche well).

Lulu's production charge for 6" x 9" paperbacks is $4.50 plus 2 cents per page. That comes out to $9.50 in this case. Lulu will take 20 percent of the remaining $25.50, or $5.10, leaving you with $20.40.

CreateSpace charges $1.50 plus 2 cents per page, which comes out to $6.50—a *lot* cheaper. But CreateSpace will take 20 percent of $35, or $7, reducing that difference slightly—leaving you with $21.50. That $3 difference in production charges is now down to a $1.10 difference in net revenue. In practice, it's worse than that: I've found that nearly all CreateSpace sales wind up coming through Amazon—which, in this case, will take $14 of the $35, leaving you with $14.50. Unless you can be sure sales will go directly to CreateSpace, not Amazon, you'll wind up earning *less* than with Lulu.

At that point, one other factor may come into play. Lulu *asks* you to purchase a copy before you make your book available for sale, to be sure it looks right—and that copy is exactly the same as any other copy. (You pay the production price for your own copies.) CreateSpace may require you to purchase a copy before you make your book available, and CreateSpace adds a page to that copy with a big "Proof" stamp, making the copy less desirable as a keepsake. So figure that you're out $6.50 extra, which for a very short book run may be significant.

All prices here are current as of early October 2011. They are subject to change, of course, although both Lulu and CreateSpace have tried to keep prices low and stable.

Other Factors

On one hand, CreateSpace *is* cheaper for copies you purchase—significantly so. I believe the quality is comparable, and for 6" x 9" and most other book sizes, both Lulu and CreateSpace offer you the option of 60# cream book paper, which is as nice as anything you'll find in trade paperbacks and significantly higher quality than most. (If you're used to paper for copiers and home printers, 60# is equivalent to 24# printer/copier paper, but the slightly textured cream stock is nice for books; 50# white is equivalent to 20# printer/copier paper.)

If you're *really* out to save money, you might want to cut your book down to 5.5" x 8.5" and use Lulu. That gives you the option of using its "Publisher Grade" paper—50# white, still as good as many trade paperbacks and much better than mass-market paperbacks—and paying $2.50 plus 1.8 cents per page. That same 250-page paperback would now have more pages—possibly as many as 304, if you leave the same margins—but even so it would cost less: $5.48 (for 304 pages) plus $2.50, or $8.08.

I've found Lulu's cover wizard considerably easier and more powerful and flexible than CreateSpace's cover creation routines, and Lulu's publishing process easier to follow. But both work well.

The fact that CreateSpace is part of Amazon may be a factor for some authors—either a positive or a negative one. Lulu is an independent corporation, with services in more than 40 countries at this point, founded with the express intent of supporting very short run books. The founder has said that Lulu doesn't want to produce 100 books with a million copies each: It would rather produce a million books with 100 copies each. In practice, it's apparently produced more than a million books with, generally, a lot fewer than 100 copies each.

Hardcovers and Downloads

There are other factors that might be decisive, covered in more detail in Chapter 11. If you're doing a family history, local history, or quite a few other kinds of micropublication, you might want to have a few hardcover copies—either to present to local history groups or libraries, or for a few people who really want hardcovers. If that's the case, Lulu is the only game in town: CreateSpace does not produce hardcovers.

Additionally, some people may prefer to download your book in PDF form rather than purchasing a print copy. All notebook computers can read PDFs using free software, as can most ebook readers—and a 6" x 9" book in PDF form should be quite readable on most ebook devices. While you can create ebook formats (EPUB for most readers, Kindle PRC for Kindles), that's another process and typically another project. With Lulu, offering a PDF version is a trivial step: Just set your price. Lulu takes 99 cents plus 20 percent of the difference between that and the price you set, or you can set the price to $0 and Lulu will waive the 99 cent charge. CreateSpace does not offer a similar PDF-download capability.

Making a Book Using Lulu, Step by Step

Let's go through the process of micropublishing a book—in this case using Lulu. The example I use is a real book: You can buy it if you're interested in Library 2.0 or just want to see the outcome of this process. Sections of screens, captured with Windows' Snipping Tool and converted to grayscale with Word's picture tools, are chosen to be as clear as possible while taking up as little space as possible.

This process assumes you've already created a Lulu account (and a PayPal account if you don't already have one) and logged in.

Starting the Project

You need to be logged in to your Lulu account. Click on the Publish tab on the homepage (or Start a New Project from your my Lulu page) and click on Start publishing your book.

That takes you to an intermediate page that describes the sizes, binding options, and paper options available. If you scroll down that page, you'll find a table of book specifications, each row of which includes a downloadable .zip file of templates—cover templates and Word body template—for that particular size. You may find the templates useful or you may not. In any case, you need to click on one of several yellow Start Publishing buttons, all of which take you to the first actual step. Click on Make a Paperback Book to keep going.

Title, Author, and Initial Availability

The first thing you do is name the project by providing a working title for your book, as shown in Figure 9.2. Lulu fills in the author name from your account, but you can change it at this point. Lulu also prompts Keep it private and accessible only to me as an initial project status, on the assumption that you'll want to review a proof copy before you open the book for sale. (If your micropublication is one where you will be buying all the copies and distributing or reselling them, you can leave the project in this status permanently.)

As with every remaining step, you need to click Save & Continue to proceed. As soon as you click this the first time, Lulu creates a project—a book, although it's not ready yet.

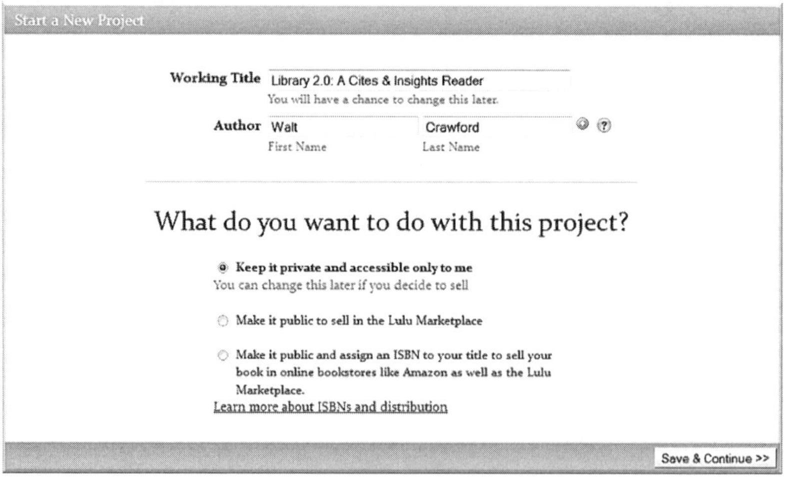

Figure 9.2 Title, author, and initial availability

Printing Options

The **Options** step (not shown) is where you choose paper, book size, binding, and whether the inside of the book is full color or black and white. The selection is shown by a yellow background for the selected option. The defaults are **Publisher Grade, U.S. Letter, Perfect-bound,** and **Black and White.** For this book, I changed the paper to **Standard** (60# cream paper) and the book size from U.S. Letter to **U.S. Trade (6" x 9" paperback).** I retained the perfect-bound and black-and-white defaults and clicked **Save & Continue.**

Uploading Your Book

It's time to upload your PDF—noting that you can pause a project at any time and come back to it later. As shown in Figure 9.3 (partial), I've used the **Browse** button to browse my computer for the file I want (using a standard file dialog box), and now I'll click **Upload.**

When you click on Upload, the window expands to show the upload process, tracking the progress of the upload. In this case, it took about as long to upload a 4.9 MB PDF as it did to write this paragraph, maybe 90 seconds in all over 1.5 Mb DSL broadband.

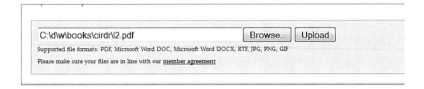

Figure 9.3 Upload step

At the end of the upload process—usually just a few minutes, although I've seen it take half an hour for a long book (with lots of photos) with a PDF larger than 50 MB—you get one of two messages at the top of the screen. The one you *don't* want to get tells you there are problems with your PDF, most typically due to typefaces that weren't embedded. What you *hope* to see is the message "Your file has been added to your book successfully." You've succeeded: Your PDF meets Lulu's standards.

It's possible to upload more than one PDF for the body of your book and let Lulu combine them, but most of the time you'll have one single file that you control. This page, instead of a **Save & Continue** button, has a different button: **Make Print-Ready File.** Click on that button.

After Lulu creates a print-ready file, it will encourage you to download and review your file, which really isn't necessary unless you're combining more than one source file. It also offers various paid extras to improve your book. You can cheerfully ignore those offers and click either of two **Save & Continue** buttons. Lulu now knows the size of your book—209 pages in this case—based on the successful creation of the print-ready file.

Creating a Cover

There are three different cover wizards (one dedicated to one-piece wraparound covers), and you can also choose options that allow you to upload prepared front and back covers.

For this example, I used the new cover wizard—choosing a background, a better layout, and a theme, and then modifying the typefaces and adding text on the back cover. Lulu provides the front cover and spine text based on project information and chooses a default typeface. You can change any or all of those elements as you proceed.

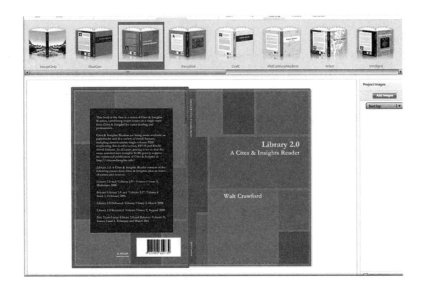

Figure 9.4 Completed cover in Lulu Cover Wizard

I found a theme that suited my needs (for now) and that theme provides colors and typefaces, although I chose to change the typeface to
Garamond. Double-click on an area showing text in order to modify that
text (in my case, eliminating a colon and breaking the subtitle to a separate line, as well as changing typeface and size). For the text box on the
back cover, the cover wizard includes a rudimentary text editor, and you
can copy and paste text from other sources (as I did here for the five
source essays in this compilation book). The results appear in Figure 9.4.

This screen has a **Preview & Make Print-Ready Cover** button,
which takes you to a screen where almost all the space is used to show
your cover. From that screen, you can click **Edit Your Cover** to go back
to the editing window or **Make Your Print-Ready Cover** to have Lulu
generate a cover PDF. When you do the latter, you get an intermediate
screen asking for patience while the cover generator works, saying it may
take a few minutes. In this case, it took no more than 10 to 15 seconds, not
really long enough to do a screen capture.

You get another invitation to download and review your book
cover, your book interior, or both. Then **Save & Continue**. This will
take you to the next step, shown in Figure 9.5—a full review of your
project's status.

Figure 9.5 Project review page before description

Ready for Proofing Order

You're almost ready for the proofing stage. Note that the button now says **Save & Finish**. This page shows all available information on your project, including the price you'll pay for each copy. You can't set retail prices until you make the book available for Direct Access (unusual, but may be suitable if you *only* want people you know to be able to buy copies) or General Access. Lulu does *not* require you to buy a proof copy before you make the book generally available. If you're confident that things are how you want them to be, you can click **Change**, modify **Availability**, and add prices and other information. Otherwise, you'll come back to revise your project after buying and checking a proof copy (which, in this case, costs $8.68). Depending on where you click **Change** and

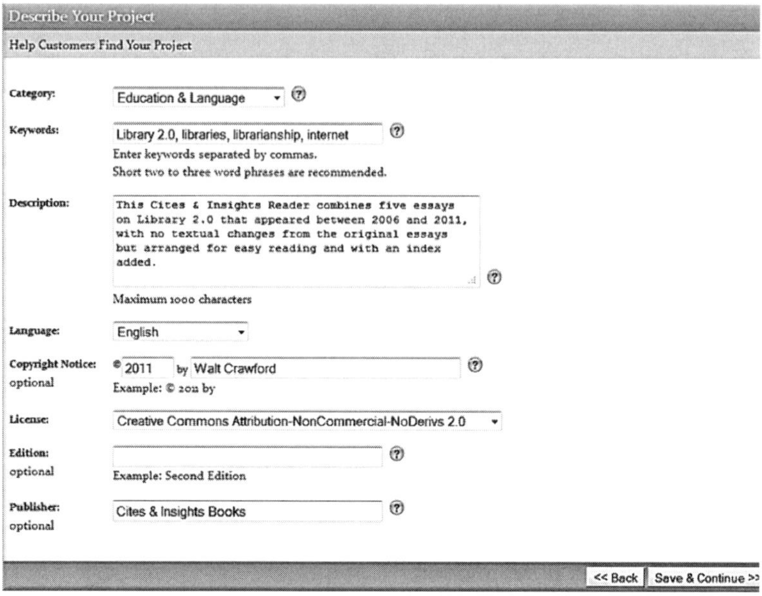

Figure 9.6 Describing your project

whether you change things from here or from your project list, you may have to go through the early steps again—but you can keep clicking **Save & Finish** at each step until you get to the new ones.

Description

Here, you must select one of Lulu's book categories and can add keywords, a description of your book (which will appear on your book page), and add other settings if you choose—including adding a Creative Commons license from the **License** pull-down. Figure 9.6 shows this page after I added information appropriate for this book.

Pricing and Completion

The next screen, shown in Figure 9.7, lets you set a price, beginning with the defaults. In this case, since I want a minimum of $4 revenue, I

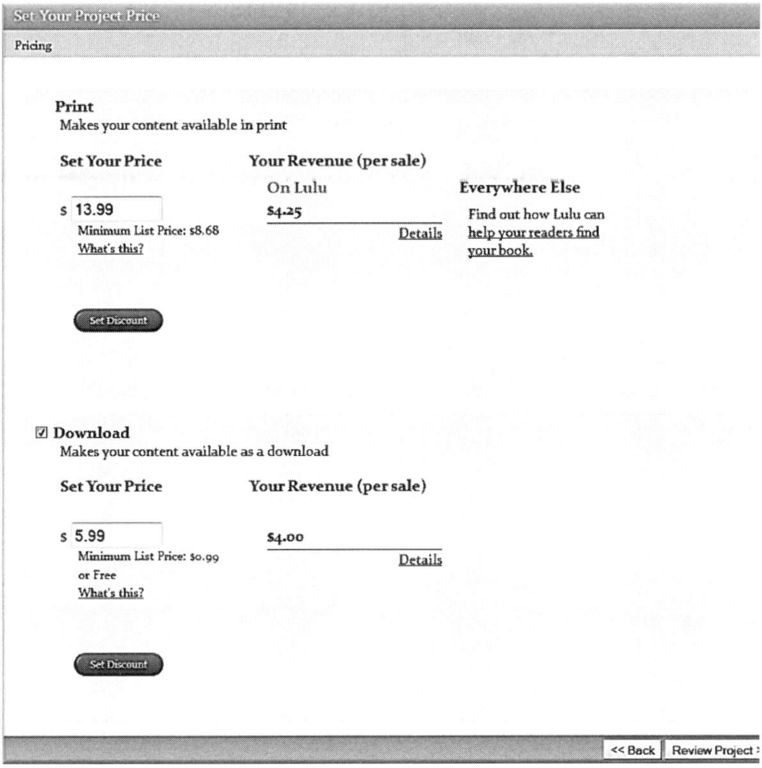

Figure 9.7 Setting your project price

set the price at the nearest 99-cent increment that gets me that much—
$13.99 for the paperback, $5.99 for a PDF download.

Now click **Review Project**, which yields a screen similar to Figure
9.5 but with your description filled in as a Project Information section.
Click on **Save and Finish** again, and you should get a screen similar
to Figure 9.8.

There it is—the book is published. You'll probably want to purchase
a copy, and you'll also want to view and possibly customize the preview that's available from your title page. The link for the title takes you
directly to that title page, a clean page showing the details of your book
(and allowing for reader reviews). The automatic preview consists of
the front cover, the first 10 pages of the book itself, and the back cover.
Lulu also creates an "Author Spotlight" that provides information about

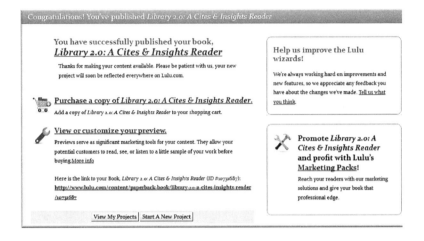

Figure 9.8 Project completion page

all your books and easy order buttons for print and downloadable copies. You can customize your Author Spotlight, but that's getting into marketing. For now, you're done.

It took about an hour to go through all these steps along with writing up this section and editing the screen captures—but plan to spend a day or two getting things just the way you want them.

Lulu will send you an email informing you that you've successfully published a book and suggesting some other steps. That email will contain the URL you use to send people directly to your book's page, just as the completion step showed you that URL. People can also search on Lulu for your book by title or author.

Differences When Using CreateSpace

The CreateSpace process is generally similar, but the steps are slightly different and there are a couple of significant differences:

➤ Instead of paying you via PayPal, CreateSpace pays directly into your bank account, so you'll have to provide details of an appropriate account. As with Lulu, CreateSpace pays monthly.

➤ CreateSpace requires that you purchase a proof copy before your book can be made available for sale and stamps that copy as a proof copy (although that requirement may be changing). If you need to make any revisions, you must purchase a new proof copy each and every time.

➢ Unless you decide otherwise, CreateSpace books automatically show up on Amazon eventually. Lulu books for which you haven't purchased distribution plans *may* show up on Amazon, but there's no guarantee.

➢ CreateSpace doesn't have individual author highlight pages or storefronts. Your book's description will be available along with ordering instructions reachable via a direct URL, but there's no way to cluster several books together.

➢ CreateSpace does not offer PDF downloads as an ebook option. It will, however, point you to the Kindle self-publishing process.

➢ CreateSpace considers your portion of sales to be royalties and will send you a 1099 at the end of the year—and, of course, report your royalties to the IRS. Lulu assumes that you're the publisher and Lulu is providing a service, so it's up to you to declare net book sales as income on your Schedule C. There's no 1099.

➢ If you decide you're going to sell lots of copies of your book, CreateSpace has a ProPlan, costing $39 and $5 per year for each book. You get even better pricing with ProPlan—lower fixed charges (an 85-cent setup charge plus 1.2 cents per page).

With CreateSpace as with Lulu, *take your time* and you'll do just fine.

10
Beyond Text Paperbacks

Up to now, we've been discussing the book form best suited to low-cost/no-cost micropublishing: trade paperbacks consisting of black-and-white text with full-color covers, possibly including black-and-white graphics.

That description includes almost all fiction and a majority of non-fiction. Your needs and desires might require more. Let's look at some possibilities and what they'll mean for your micropublication.

Hardcover Books

If you use Lulu and your book is either 6" x 9" (the standard trade paper-back size) or 8.5" x 11" (American full-page size), you can create a hard-cover version of your book with very little difficulty—but it will come at a price. (For proof of concept, see the hardcover edition of this book available through Lulu.)

Lulu can convert paperbacks directly to hardcover in these two sizes. In the case of 6" x 9" books, it's a trivial conversion, as the book pages are still 6" x 9" and the cover's expanded to a 6.25" x 9.25" binding. (I've only done casewrap books, where the cover is part of the binding. Dust jacket books, with plain navy blue linen covers and separate dust jackets, may involve different rules.) In the case of converting 8.5" x 11" books, it works the other way around: The pages shrink slightly in the conversion process while the cover stays the same. In both cases, the results are excellent.

The prices aren't so excellent. As of early October 2011, a 6" x 9" casewrap book costs $13 plus 2 cents per page—in other words, you pay an extra $8.50 for the extra binding step. That's outrageous by traditional publishing standards, but it's possibly reasonable given that this is one-at-a-time binding with full-color covers. Dust jacket books cost a dollar more: $14 plus 2 cents per page. The premium for hardcover seems to fluctuate, but it's a significant premium.

For 8.5" x 11" books, it's worse—but that's true for paperbacks as well, where Lulu's prices have gone up to $5.50 plus 2.5 cents per page (unless you use 50# "publisher grade" paper, in which case it's $3.50 plus 1.8 cents per page). You can't use publisher grade paper for a casewrap 8.5" x 11" book, and as of October 2011, the binding charge is also higher for 8.5" x 11" than it is for 6" x 9"—$15 instead of $13.

Running the numbers, this means that a 250-page 6" x 9" book, which has a production cost of $9.50 as a trade paperback, will have a production cost of $18 as a casewrap book, but that might be worthwhile for some copies of your book. For a 250-page 8.5" x 11" book, the production cost goes from $11.75 for paperback to $21.25 for casewrap.

Other Bindings

There may be cases in which your book would work better with Plasti-Coil binding (plastic spiral spine), as that allows the book to lie flat at any pair of pages. Lulu also offers that option for quite a few book sizes; it costs an extra $1.50 above typical paperback prices.

For books with relatively few pages, you might want saddle-stitched binding ("stapled" is such an ordinary word!). That may be your best option for very short books or booklets (which really don't make much economic sense via Lulu, given the high initial charge). Saddle-stitched books can be any multiple of four pages from four to 88 pages, while perfect-bound books must be at least 32 pages long (and at least 70 to 80 pages long for the spine to be thick enough for the title and author to appear). Very short books can also use Plasti-Coil binding, which allows four to 400 pages in typical page sizes. By comparison, perfect-bound books can run anywhere from 32 to 740 pages, and casewrap (hardbound) books can be as short as 24 pages and as long as 800 pages.

All CreateSpace books are perfect-bound paperbacks. The page range is 24 to 740 pages (for most page sizes; up to 570 for 8.5" x 11") for cream paper, 24 to 808 (650 for 8.5" x 11") for white paper.

Photos

You can include photos in your book—but don't expect miracles. Black-and-white books are printed on high-speed laser printers, which are never ideal for photographic output, and the cream book paper that looks best for most books has a slight texture that can make photos a little trickier. You can opt for white paper, which may improve photo quality a little, but that still won't make it anything close to the quality of the glossy insert pages you see in some traditional books, or even high-quality offset lithography on good book paper.

Glossy inserts are not currently possible using micropublishing providers. They require extra steps in the printing-and-binding process that don't work for one-at-a-time production at reasonable prices.

You *can* take steps to make your photos come out as crisp as possible. These mostly consist of convincing Microsoft Word and, if you're using a PDF generation program, PDF not to downgrade your photos.

The basic rules are these:

➤ Photos should have 300 dpi resolution. For a picture that's as wide as the page (26 picas or 4.33" for this book template), the horizontal resolution should be 1,300 pixels.

➤ Photos should be grayscale. Do the conversion from color yourself. (Word's internal image editing tools will handle this: Just reduce color saturation to 0 percent.)

➤ Do *not* use Word's compression routines for photos, as the highest resolution provided is 220 dpi.

➤ Tell Word not to downgrade your images. Go into **Options** from the **File** tab, choose **Advanced**, scroll down to **Image Size and Quality**, and check the box **Do not compress images in file**, as shown in Figure 10.1. (Then click **OK**.)

➤ If you're using a PDF printer-equivalent to produce your PDF, go into the options pages and ensure that settings for images are at least 300 dpi. The location of these settings will vary from program to program.

Those rules should yield reasonably good photo quality. If you need better photographic quality, then you'll need to use a different kind of book production, as discussed in the next section.

Figure 10.1 Image Size and Quality setting

Color and True Photo Quality

Both Lulu and CreateSpace offer full-color interior printing—for a price. The price may make you gasp, particularly when you realize that to have *any* color pages inside a book, the entire book must be printed using color methods.

CreateSpace prints color books on 60# white paper and offers most of the same choices for book size as for black-and-white books. Page costs jump to 12 cents per page—so, for example, a 100-page book would cost $13.75 to produce, and a 200-page book would cost $25.75.

Lulu uses 80# matte-finish white paper, a heavier stock designed for full-color printing—and charges more as well. Page costs jump to 20 cents per page (binding charges are the same). So a 100-page book would cost $24.50 to produce; a 200-page book would cost $44.50. I haven't used either service for color books, but I would expect Lulu's books to look significantly nicer.

If you want the *best* photo quality, you're in a different realm; a number of other companies such as Blurb also offer book production services with no initial charges but high per-book charges. Lulu has offerings in this area, including large-format coffee-table books printed on 100# silk finish paper—but at $29.95 setup plus 75 cents per page, this is clearly out of the realm of low-cost micropublishing. You'd want to investigate a range of service providers and look for user testimonials before you attempt this level of photo quality.

The short version: Adding interior color is going to be much more expensive for each book—and if what you need is a photo book of coffee-table or art book quality, whether black-and-white or color, you're dealing with a different set of issues than those covered in this book.

Ebooks

If you're micropublishing for a narrow, well-known audience, you probably know whether there's a desire for ebook formats and, if so, which ones. Assuming you've already created a Word document as your book's body and a PDF for Lulu or CreateSpace, one standard format is trivially easy (no work at all!), and two should be easier than they are as of this writing.

The three common ebook formats considered here are:

➤ PDF, the most portable and the only ebook format that will fully retain your formatting

➤ EPUB, the so-called industry standard ebook format, used on almost all ebook readers with one notable exception: the Kindle

➤ Kindle PRC, a variant form of Mobipocket's MOBI format, used on the Kindle and, in the Mobipocket variant, several other places

PDF: Just Do It

Using Lulu for your paperback or hardcover book? When you get to the point of telling Lulu how your book can be sold and what you're charging for it, you have the option of adding a PDF download price. If you choose the options that allow PDF downloads, Lulu supports them. That's all there is to it. You saw the process in the previous chapter—the *default* is to add a PDF download.

Lulu charges 99 cents for PDF downloads and takes the usual 20 percent of the difference between that and your retail price. So if you price a PDF at $10.99, you'll get $8. There's one exception: If you want to *give away* the download, which can be a great way to promote your book, set the PDF price to $0 and Lulu waives its 99 cent charge. If you believe giving away the ebook is a great way to promote the print book, Lulu makes that easy.

Since you hold the copyright and all rights to the PDF you uploaded to Lulu (except the rights to an ISBN that Lulu provided), you can also make that PDF available from your own website, an institutional repository, or anywhere else that suits your needs. ISBN aside, *it's your book* and you can do with it as you please.

My sense is that 6" x 9" books with suitable margins should display nicely as PDFs on any notebook, tablet, desktop, or ebook reader with at least a 7" screen. They won't work very well on smartphones, iPod Touch, and other devices with small screens: For those, you need an ebook format that reflows text. On the other hand, PDFs display the typefaces and layout that you chose and worked to get right.

For what it's worth, the PDF/A produced directly from Word *does* support accessibility features, including text-to-speech technology. Unfortunately, in my tests using Adobe Reader X, text-to-speech isn't great: It works but gets confused by hyphenation and other factors. Still, it's there and it's enabled.

The PDFs you produce in Word and make available for download from Lulu will not have Digital Rights Management (DRM) protections built in. There may be ways to add DRM restrictions, but I see no reason why you'd consider them.

EPUB: Theoretically Not Difficult

Most ebook readers support the EPUB format, with or without DRM. You can find books on how to prepare EPUB files, but the one I read was mostly about HTML editing and would frighten away most casual users. I don't believe you need go to all that trouble.

There may be add-ons to Word that will allow you to generate EPUB files directly. At this writing, the one I've seen doesn't work for Word 2010, but that may be resolved.

An earlier draft of this book described a simple process to get from your Word document to an EPUB book. Here's the process—but I can't say it will get you all the way there, although I believe the steps are the right ones.

➢ First, simplify your document slightly—primarily by removing running headers and footers. EPUB is inherently a flowed format: The number of pages in an EPUB book depends entirely on the size of the reader screen and the type size used by the person reading the book. A 250-page print book may be a 400-page ebook for one person, a 500-page ebook for the next. More to the point, running headers will confuse EPUB generation programs. Leave the table of contents, as it will be useful.

➢ Now, save the resulting document—but as filtered HTML, not as a .doc or .docx file. The option shows up as **Web Page, Filtered** in the pull-down menu on the **Save As** dialog box. This creates an .htm file.

➢ You'll also want to generate a simple cover. I've seen suggestions to create a cover that's 1,600 x 1,200 pixels or 1,800 x 1,200 pixels; in any case, the cover should be simple and include title and author. Save that as a JPEG or other graphics file.

Now you *should* be able to use a conversion program or website to turn the HTML file and your cover into a proper EPUB file, ready to upload to ebook stores. Unfortunately, the conversion program I've seen recommended most often—Calibre—has one big advantage and a bigger disadvantage.

The big advantage: It's free (from calibre-ebook.com) and open source, and it's also an ebook library management program with a built-in ebook viewer to simulate readers. You can also use it to sync ebooks with your own ebook reader. When I tried converting a Word book modified as above, the results looked really good—in Calibre's simulated reader.

The disadvantage: The EPUB file I created using Calibre was not acceptable to Lulu's EPUB wizard: It doesn't meet required standards for full EPUB compatibility. As a result, I can't honestly say that I've managed to create a proper EPUB. I suspect that tools for creating validated EPUB files will become more robust over time and that you may soon find it easy to create such files directly from Word.

The whole ebook marketplace is in sort of a Wild West phase as this is written. Once things settle down—which would ideally mean Kindle accepting EPUB files and the various bookstores settling on a single set of requirements—you can expect Calibre and other tools to produce the files you need without difficulty. Right now, that's chancier.

But we're getting there: In late 2011, Lulu began offering free conversion from Word to EPUB, but for the conversion to work properly, you must carry out an extensive process of downgrading and eliminating formatting.

Kindle: Theoretically Not Much More Difficult

If you already have Calibre, you can make a MOBI file just as easily as you can make an EPUB file—it's another conversion option. In my brief tests, the output didn't seem to be as good as with EPUB, although it's certainly still usable. (The differences: Bullets didn't come out as well, and it made bad assumptions about typefaces, in this case assuming that headings as well as body text were in serif type.)

From what I've been told, the way to get to Kindle's PRC file from a MOBI file is simply to *rename the extension* (from .mobi to .prc) using Windows Explorer or the Mac equivalent.

Amazon's Kindle Direct Publishing will also accept either MOBI or EPUB files directly and convert them to the PRC format. Amazon's royalty rate after a delivery charge of 15 cents is 70 percent for U.S. (and some other countries) sales of ebooks priced from $2.99 to $9.99, and 35 percent for other sales, so a $9.99 book would yield $6.88 when purchased by U.S. customers.

Again, I haven't actually tried this. I can say that it should work; I can't prove that it will work. Since the EPUB file didn't work and Kindle Direct Publishing broke partway through setting up an account, the reality may be as poor for Kindle as it is for EPUB.

In both cases, we'll get there—but maybe not for a while yet.

If and when I find free conversion methods that demonstrably work properly, I'll identify them on the website for this book (see "About the Website").

11
Marketing and Publicity
—and Making It Big

If you plan to move beyond micropublishing (where the goal is to produce a few books for a targeted niche that you already know how to reach), you'll probably spend more time and money on marketing and publicity than on any other aspect of publishing.

There are many books and other resources (including thousands of blogs and other websites) about marketing and publicity. Your library almost certainly has books that will help you with marketing, including books on self-publishing. Most of the books I've seen about self-publishing spend more time and attention on marketing than on any other topic. That may be appropriate. Some go so far as to say that you shouldn't even *write* a book until you've done the market research to be sure you can sell hundreds of copies. That might be true for traditional self-publishing, and that may be one thing that separates traditional self-publishing from micropublishing.

Helpful Tips for Marketing and Publicity

Marketing and publicity cover everything from the description you write for your book page on Lulu or CreateSpace to setting up an author tour, improbable as that may be for a micropublished book. Following are a few of the things you might want to think about—the first few related to micropublishing as well as larger-scale self-publishing. You almost certainly need to plan for the first three steps and possibly the first four; the rest may be irrelevant for a micropublication.

127

Identify Your Customers

Who should buy your book? You should already have your short list and an even shorter list of people you'll be giving copies to. If it's the right kind of book, your local history society, genealogy society, or the history room at the library may want a copy—preferably a donated casewrap copy.

Is there a larger list of potential customers—people who might like the book if they knew about it? That's a tougher question, but one you should certainly investigate.

You should *not* assume that your public library will buy a copy or even accept and retain one as a donation. Unless the library has the space and policies to support a strong local-author collection, the library may not be in a position to keep your book—even if the library helped you produce it. It doesn't hurt to ask about your public library's policies for local authors, but it's not realistic to assume that the library will or can automatically add micropublished books to its collection.

As you develop lists of people who you believe should buy your book and groups of people who might find it interesting, temper possibility with reality. A lot of people who *might* find your book worthwhile aren't interested in buying it. But you may find unlikely candidates lined up as buyers—if you can reach them.

Identify the Competition

Your book should be the best of its kind, shouldn't it? If it duplicates the subject and approach of another book and it's not better than the other book in some way, why bother writing and publishing it? Certainly not for the money, not if you're micropublishing, and preferably not just because you want your name on a book: There are easier ways to boost your ego.

But your definition of "its kind" may be quite narrow, and that may be appropriate. Chances are, there are related books—that's likely to be true even for family histories. It doesn't hurt to be aware of those books. They may not be direct competition, but they're competitors for people's time and money. If you know the competition, you're in a better position to identify what makes your book different and (for some readers) better, and to communicate that to potential customers.

Reach Your Customers

The greatest book in the world is useless if nobody knows about it. The Lulu Marketplace has too many books in it to mean much in terms of reaching customers—and even though Google will probably pick up references to your book, that may not do much good.

You need to let your customers know about your book and why they should buy it. That's true for the short list of sure-thing customers and for the much larger list of potential customers.

There are many ways to reach your customers without traditional and expensive marketing campaigns. Social networks expand your options. By using email, Facebook, Twitter, Google+, your blog (if you have one), and other online options, you should be able to get the word out to many people who should know about your book.

Play fair. Pay attention to restrictions on commercial postings. For example, genealogy lists may explicitly forbid advertisements, but it might be appropriate to simply announce your new book. Don't spam people. Keep your messages clear and concise but not necessarily identical. You're not creating sales pitches; you're letting people know there's something they may find valuable—and why they'll find it valuable.

Sell Your Books at Personal Appearances

If you speak from time to time, it may be appropriate to sell your books at the same venue—if you have help to handle transactions at the back of the room after you speak.

You can and should mention your book (if the speech is related) and possibly have cards or include information in your handouts giving the book's summary and URL for ordering. Selling physical copies on the spot is more complicated. You'll need to order multiple copies (probably getting a price break in the process—for Lulu, at least, you'll get 5 percent off production costs for five copies, 10 percent off for 15, and 15 percent off for 30). You may find that you now have inventory, which may require a different tax status and accounting method for your IRS 1099 Schedule C and may require a city business license (or a different license). And, of course, you have to handle cash and probably credit cards. For a true micropublication, this may be more trouble than it's worth, but it can also be a way to sell a fair number of books, moving from micropublishing to self-publishing.

Issue a Press Release

Now we get into more traditional self-publishing marketing, much of which you'll never do as a micropublisher. At this point, if this and the following subheads seem like things you should be doing, you need to read other resources on marketing in general and marketing books in particular. The section "Some Useful Resources," later in this chapter, includes some candidates, but there are many others.

There are two parts to a good press release: writing it so it works, and sending it to the right places. There's little question that a well-written press release can show up, word for word, as a story on various websites and in community newspapers. You should investigate how good press releases work and think about the message you want to send, which is never simply "Buy my book!"

Finding and building the right mailing list is possibly one of the most important tasks in moving from micropublishing to broader self-publishing. Pay attention to resources and decide whether it's worth buying targeted mailing lists.

Send Out Review Copies

Hope to have libraries buy copies of your book? Other than your own library, and frequently even then, you're unlikely to have much luck—unless the book has been reviewed in a reputable publication.

Targeted review copies can yield a variety of benefits. A specialty periodical in the field you're writing about might give you a great writeup—and somebody else's review of your book has more credibility than your own letter or article about why it's great. You hope to see a variety of reviews for your book on Amazon, on Lulu, and elsewhere. Don't be discouraged if somebody writes a negative or even stupid review: To some extent, bad reviews *also* sell books.

But sending out review copies is expensive and time-consuming. You have to find out who should get copies, you have to buy copies, and you have to package and ship review copies with your press release enclosed. Figure about $4 per copy in addition to the book itself, and consider that you might have to send out 40 or 50 copies to yield one or two reviews. For a true micropublication, one or two targeted review copies may make more sense.

You can *buy* reviews (books on self-publishing will tell you where), but I doubt that it's a wise expenditure. Paid reviews have very little credibility, at least for libraries, but you can quote them on Amazon, and that might be worth something.

One problem with some major review publications, quite apart from their general inability to cope with the sheer flood of self-published books and micropublications, is that they usually want to see a galley version of a book several months before it's actually published. You can do that, to be sure (use a dummy cover, retain private status for your book, and send those versions out as review and advance reading copies), but do you really want to keep your book out of readers' hands for an extra three to six months?

Try to Get Media Coverage

Think a radio station (either over-the-air or internet radio) will interview you about the book? Given the growth of podcasts and internet radio, that's still possible, even as the homogenization of broadcast radio has reduced the number of truly local radio outlets.

If you have the right story to tell and you're willing to spend the time and money to tell it, you could get on the radio, possibly even TV (at least a local cable access channel). You could certainly get into local weekly newspapers and specialized publications. Only you can decide whether the possible reward is worth the effort.

Aim for Bookstores

If you've written a book on local history, about local trails, or even about families within the community, chances are your local bookstores will carry the book—with caveats.

First, they'll probably want you to supply a small number of copies at a heavy discount from the price you want them to charge (say 40 percent as a minimal discount).

Second, many of them won't touch the book unless it has an ISBN.

Third and worst, nearly all of them will insist on returnability for full credit and may not pay for the books in advance—so after two months, you may have a stack of shelf-worn books, unsuitable for sale anywhere else, and little or no revenue.

Finally, it's up to you to publicize the book. Bookstores deal with a huge variety of books and can only feature a few of them.

Is it worth it? Only you can make that decision.

Find Non-Traditional Sales Outlets

Depending on your book's topic, there may be other stores that will sell it—some of them eagerly. If you've written a book about local hiking trails, sporting goods stores might carry it, just as one example. Stores that aren't primarily bookstores probably won't care about an ISBN, but they *will* want some form of stock number (which they may assign). The stores will want a discounted wholesale price—but, in many cases, they'll pay you for the books and will *not* expect to be able to return them for credit, since most other merchandise doesn't work that way.

For the right book in the right area, this can be a boon, but you're still in the self-publishing position of buying bunches of books, taking them around to stores, and acting as a merchant.

There are, of course, many online sales outlets in addition to physical stores. Lulu and CreateSpace are only too happy to make your books available through other distributors—for a price or at least a discount. Look at what they offer; determine whether it's worthwhile.

Advertise

I can think of very few cases in which you'd pay for advertising for a micropublication. The potential added sales would rarely recoup the costs, much less yield additional profit. But if you really believe you can sell hundreds or thousands of copies, you might consider advertising in appropriate offline and online media. Do targeted online ads make sense for you? Can you justify a small ad in the local weekly?

Never Stop

The ultimate lesson in serious book marketing: *It never stops.* You're *always* selling yourself and your book. If that gives you the willies, maybe you're better off sticking with micropublishing, where the financial rewards are minimal but the psychic cost is also minimal.

Some Useful Resources

I looked at a number of books as sources of advice on aspects of self-publishing and, in most cases, as *examples* of self-publishing. In a public library that uses the Dewey Decimal System, go to 070.593 and see what's available, and then look for other books in different areas on marketing and publicity in general.

In the case of book design, I'm satisfied that the tools and advice offered in this book will result in *your* book being considerably more professional and finished in appearance than most self-published books I've seen, including those from vanity or subsidy publishers such as the many imprints of AuthorHouse.

But some self-publishers have done well, so their advice on marketing and publicity may be worth paying attention to—if you believe strong marketing will be worthwhile.

The Economical Guide to Self-Publishing: How to Produce and Market Your Book On a Budget by Linda Foster Radke, self-published by her Five Star Publications

Radke's advice on marketing may be useful, much as it pains me to read that simply self-publishing any book on a topic makes you into an instant expert who will be in demand by radio stations. I don't believe it's quite that easy.

The Complete Idiot's Guide to Self-Publishing by Jennifer Basye Sander, published by Alpha Books

This one's chock-full of good advice, except in a few cases, such as Sander's dismissal of laser printing and TrueType. She offers useful caveats, real numbers on costs, and a huge amount of advice on marketing, the key to successful self-publishing beyond micropublishing.

Dan Poynter's Self-Publishing Manual by Dan Poynter, self-published by Para Publishing

Poynter is clearly successful, and he has useful advice about marketing possibilities if you're determined to sell thousands of copies of your book. It helps a *lot* if you believe all nonfiction books are how-to books, as Poynter apparently does, and if you can tolerate repetition and a jackhammer prose style, along with an animus for publishers and a view of POD providers that's only accurate if you wholly ignore the existence of Lulu and CreateSpace—which Poynter does.

The Complete Self-Publishing Handbook by David M. Brownstone and Irene M. Franck, published by Plume

The calm discussion in this book is a refreshing change of pace—and it's notable that this book on self-publishing is *not* self-published.

Much of the advice on marketing is good. The detailed comments on actual costs appear sound. The authors are, I believe, far too conservative on copyright (they use scare quotes around fair use and basically advise ignoring it) and wrongly suggest that black ink on white paper (not cream) is how "almost all" books are printed and the most readable combination. This book is an odd combination of trade paperback pricing ($13.95 in 1999 dollars) and mass-market appearance (low-grade paper, 5.2" x 8" size), but it's a good introduction.

Making It Big: Beyond Micropublishing

What happens when your little book becomes a big hit—when you find that you've moved from a few dozen copies to several hundred, with the potential for hundreds or thousands more?

Since we're dreaming here, let's dream *big*: In addition to the handful of print copies you needed, you offered your book as a PDF download for $2.99 or as an ebook for $2.99 or $4.99, and it's done so well that a publisher has contacted you and wants to pick up the book for its publisher's list.

What now? Do you accept the publisher's proposal? *Can* you accept the publisher's proposal? (That final question is particularly relevant if you chose to use some of the other possible ways to produce a small number of books—"publishers" who assert rights to your book.)

The Good News: You Own the Rights

For both Lulu and CreateSpace, with the exception of an ISBN the provider has assigned you and the possible exception of the book cover, there's no question. You own the rights to your book and are perfectly free to take it elsewhere—either removing it from Lulu or CreateSpace or continuing to sell it there. That's how I've been able to publish three books on both Lulu and CreateSpace, and it's the fundamental truth if you find that a book has grown beyond micropublishing. You don't have to negotiate with your provider; you don't even have to tell the provider.

You may need one change in the new edition. If your book has an ISBN provided by Lulu or CreateSpace, the version you publish elsewhere needs a new ISBN. If an existing publisher picks up your book, it will assign an ISBN from its range in any case.

Bulk Purchases and Other Channels

The per-copy production price for Lulu and CreateSpace books is high compared to traditional printing—except that you don't get good prices from traditional printers unless you're printing at least 1,000 copies.

For intermediate runs, say more than 100 copies and fewer than 1,000, your first option should be to see how much your provider will charge. Lulu offers quotations for bulk purchases from 250 to 2,500 copies—using print on demand techniques for up to 1,000 copies, with the option of traditional offset printing for larger quantities. For purchases of fewer than 250 copies, Lulu has rising quantity discounts.

Lulu and CreateSpace can both make your books available through additional channels—in some cases with restrictions, in some cases with lower production costs. Additional channels may include bookstore purchases, still with Lulu or CreateSpace taking a share of the proceeds for their services.

Traditional Self-Publishing

If you're going great guns, it may make financial sense to become a self-publisher, using traditional printers to produce your books. That requires that you have an appropriate business license; space to store all those books; the willingness to handle shipments, returns, and billing; and enough capital to pay for a run of 1,000 or more copies. At that point, if you don't already have an imprint name, you'll want to create one, making sure it's not already used and, for most jurisdictions, doing the advertising and submissions necessary for a fictitious business name. Once you're self-publishing, you might even become a "real publisher" by publishing the work of other authors. By now, you're way beyond anything this book can cover.

Other Publishers

Yes, a few publishers have published books that were previously only available through Lulu or as ebooks. No, it doesn't happen often.

If you're approached with an offer, you need to make sure you're dealing with a real publisher (not a vanity press willing to help you out for a large additional fee) and that the numbers make sense to you. For a given sales level, you'll make more by staying on your own—but you'll also spend more time and energy in the process.

If you're in this fortunate situation, you might consider a counter-offer: If the publisher thinks your work is so great, will it give you a good advance for your *next* book or for a substantially revised new edition of your existing book? In that case, you can gain the advantages of a good publisher—professional editing, professional copyediting, professional layout and typography, professional indexing, professional cover design, and professional distribution and marketing—without giving up the larger per-copy revenue you're getting from your micropublication or self-published books. Good publishers add talent and prestige; don't ignore those values.

Stick With It

For some of you, the Lulu or CreateSpace route may continue to make sense even if sales climb into the thousands. You could print ten or fifty copies at a time to sell through a local store while having most of your sales handled by your provider. Consider the alternatives. Consider your comfort level with aspects of publishing and marketing. And, to be sure, enjoy your success! The problems of coping with a micropublication that has suddenly sold 1,000 copies are problems most of us would love to have.

12
Academic Libraries and Micropublishing: Ejournals in Print Form

Most of this book concerns public libraries and their communities. That's not to say academic libraries, especially smaller ones, may not find it worthwhile. A few words about libraries as publishers may be useful here; then we'll look at one special case where libraries can effectively use micropublishing tools: making small ejournals available in print form without much extra labor or any new funds.

Academic Libraries as Publishers

I've assumed that academic libraries and their parent institutions typically have the advanced software and access to professional talent to handle most publishing-related tasks, but that may not always be the case. It does seem likely that more and more academic libraries will be acting as publishers in the future.

SPARC has announced a "Library Publishing Services: Strategies for Success" project (www.arl.org/sparc/partnering). That project already includes *Campus-Based Publishing Partnerships: A Guide to Critical Issues*, a 73-page PDF on existing and future digital publishing programs in academic libraries and collaboration between academic libraries and university presses. That document and case studies on the site mostly involve large academic libraries. I suggest looking at the site and the documents, especially if you're in a large academic library.

What about smaller libraries—especially those in colleges and universities that don't have university presses? It may be feasible to establish a library or university imprint—primarily digital, but with print available to those wishing to pay for it—using the publishing tools and methods described in this book. If a library-based operation can establish suitable review and editorial functions and can find marketing assistance on the campus, the books themselves could be put into final form using micropublishing techniques.

More and more academic monographs *are* micropublications, with print sales never likely to reach a level that justifies printing 2,000 or even 500 copies. With a campus hosting ebook versions (or using external hosts), it's plausible to make hardcover and paperback print versions available through CreateSpace or Lulu, extending the reach and usefulness of the monographs without tying up capital.

There's a lot more to be said about ways that academic libraries can become publishers or partner with other campus agencies to publish. None of it belongs in this book. The SPARC project is one good starting point to explore the subject.

One Example: The RIT Cary Graphic Arts Press

The Cary Graphic Arts Collection at Rochester Institute of Technology (RIT) is "one of the country's premier libraries on graphic communication history and practices," according to its website at library.rit.edu/cary.

Here's the description of Cary Graphic Arts' virtual university press at RIT's store at Lulu (www.lulu.com/spotlight/carypress):

> RIT Cary Graphic Arts Press is the publication arm of the Melbert B. Cary, Jr. Graphic Arts Collection at Rochester Institute of Technology. The collection is a renowned resource for those studying printing history, bookbinding, typography, papermaking, calligraphy, and book illustration processes. Since the Cary Collection's inception in 1969, occasional publications have appeared, inspired by its holdings. Strong scholarship and editorial direction, elegant design, and fine printing have characterized these publications. With the creation of RIT Cary Graphic Arts Press, we hope to carry on these high standards and work toward the formal establishment of a university press at RIT.

As of October 2011, fifteen publications are offered, all on Lulu, including one ebook, one calendar, and two books that are also available as downloads—and, in one case, as either a $20 black-and-white paperback or a $61 full-color paperback. The collection includes one issue of the *Journal of Applied Science and Engineering Technology*, an open access journal (using Open Journal Systems software) published by the RIT Libraries in cooperation with the College of Applied Science and Technology.

New OA Journals and Micropublishing

One specific area of academic publishing seems likely to involve libraries (large and small) more and more as time goes on: open access (OA) journals, especially smaller journals in the humanities and social sciences.

If your library is interested in starting a new OA journal—or taking over an existing journal—you'll want to start with resources listed on the Open Access Directory (OAD; oad.simmons.edu/oadwiki). "Guides for OA journal publishers" is one good starting point, along with two pages linked from that page: "Free and open-source journal management software" and "OA journal business models."

A number of software systems support journal publishing. The best known is probably Open Journal Systems (OJS), a project of Public Knowledge located at pkp.sfu.ca?q=ojs.

As of October 2011, more than 10,00 titles used OJS (a partial list is available at pkp.sfu.ca/ojs-journals). Since that number is considerably larger than the *total* of gold OA journals as listed in the Directory of Open Access Journals (DOAJ), it presumably includes journals that haven't yet started publishing and journals that don't qualify for DOAJ inclusion, and, apparently, cases where OJS is being used as a publishing system for things other than journals. It's an impressive list. OJS is itself free, open source software.

OAD lists a dozen other sources for open source journal management software, including Topaz (used by the Public Library of Science).

From Online to Micropublished Print

Most new OA journals publish online as the primary and frequently sole distribution method. Frequently (I'm tempted to say *generally* but can't prove that), papers appear in PDF form.

If an OA journal has a table of contents in HTML form (as it will in almost every case), papers that are already in PDF form (usually 8.5" x 11" for U.S. journals, usually A4-size for most other countries), and—significantly—if a year's worth of papers, or a clear subset of a year's worth, totals less than 700 pages or so, the journal is a good candidate for a micropublished annual print edition. With Lulu, a micropublished print edition of an American journal can even be hardbound for library shelving. For that matter, each *issue* can be made available as a print edition, if there's demand—as long as the issue doesn't total more than 700 pages or so.

Why offer a print version? Because some libraries will want to make browsable volumes available, and because some authors will want to own bound versions of the issue or year in which their article appeared. That demand may yield half a dozen sales for a given volume, or it might yield 50 or more—in either case, not remotely enough to justify the overhead of handling print subscriptions, print runs, and distribution.

The steps are truly trivial—except for the first two steps, which need only be done once.

Step 1: Establish a Lulu Account

Lulu requires an email address and a PayPal account. That needs to be taken care of first, presumably with an official account that can accept money on behalf of the journal or the journal's sponsoring group.

Step 2: Design the Running Cover

Chances are, you'll want a single cover design for all volumes (or issues), with only the year or full date and volume/issue number changing. Since the number of pages will vary for each issue or volume, you'll want a straightforward front cover design. You might want a changing photograph for each issue or volume, depending on the desires of the editorial group. Some of the examples I've seen have used plain text on a color background.

Once you have a cover design, an editorial assistant can upload it as the front image of a simple Lulu cover for each issue or volume, with the varying type (issue or volume and date) superimposed, although it may be preferable to do the variable typography in-house on a copy of the master cover. I've seen one case where the volume and issue information appears as an author name in the Lulu listing, making an odd

Lulu page but providing an easy way to get the spine and cover right, since the cover wizard automatically includes the author's name.

Step 3: Prepare Each Issue or Volume

For this, you *do* need a PDF program that can combine many individual PDFs, which is true of most commercial PDF software. You may need to create the new PDF by printing to PDF rather than simply combining, if individual article PDFs don't have all typefaces embedded.

First, prepare a PDF for the issue or volume table of contents—easily done by importing the HTML into Microsoft Word or Libre-Office, touching it up as necessary, and creating a PDF. You can add title and copyright/Creative Commons pages at that point.

Then, stack the front matter and individual articles in your PDF program and create a single PDF file containing all of them. If you have an issue or volume index (or the time and talent to create one), it should be the final PDF in the file. Depending on the organization of the journal, you might or might not add overall running page numbers; that's certainly not a requirement. (In many cases, page numbers already run continuously through the articles in each volume.)

Step 4: Upload and Publish

That's all there is to it. Upload the body of the issue or volume. Upload the (modified) cover. Have Lulu provide spine type. Set the price, either a fixed price for each issue or volume (frequently appropriate) or a varying price depending on size.

Step 5: Add Info and URL to Journal Homepage

I've seen a number of OJS-based journals that already offer Lulu-produced print issues or volumes. It's clearly feasible to add a note on the homepage that a print version is available and to direct people to the journal's Lulu store.

Based on examples I've seen, it may be necessary to offer print issues via announcements or on a separate page; it may not be practical to add it as part of OJS-matrix issue listings. (I speak from no special knowledge, just from looking at examples.)

Not Just Theoretical

Several OA journals already offer individual issues as Lulu-produced books, with fewer offering annual volumes. This is clearly feasible and would appear to require no more than an hour or two per issue or volume. It's a nice additional service with no real risk: If nobody buys the print version, the library's not out any money.

Some examples of journals that use Lulu to offer individual issues in print form are:

➤ The *Journal of Industrial Engineering and Management*, published three times a year since 2008, uses OJS software and offers each issue separately in print form, charging $25 or more depending on issue size.

➤ The *Journal of Stuttering Therapy, Advocacy and Research* offers each issue as a minimally priced paperback (typically under $9); the process seems to be somewhat delayed.

➤ The *Asian EFL Journal* offers "hardcover" versions of some issues (including subjournals) and conference proceedings at prices ranging from $17 to $70 (in some expensive cases for full-color printing), and at least one annual collection of articles at $88 (color). Although called "hardcover," these are actually paperbacks.

➤ I already mentioned the *Journal of Applied Science and Engineering Technology* (*JASET*), published by the Rochester Institute of Technology Library and College of Applied Science and Technology; at least one issue of this OJS-based journal has appeared as a Lulu print version.

➤ The *International Journal of Modelling, Identification and Control* is now a full OA journal with author-side fees to cover costs, specializing in Nordic research activities in this field, with print issues (mostly very brief) available from Lulu at a nominal cost (typically between $5 and $6).

➤ *as|peers: emerging voices in american studies* is an annual student journal from Germany that's designed as print but also available online; it's primarily available via Lulu at $22.58 per issue (the price makes more sense in Euros), $6–$7.50 for download, for relatively slender paperbacks (e.g., 2010 is 128 pages).

A journal doesn't *need* to be open access to use Lulu for print production, although that seems the most plausible case. One remarkable exception to these typically modest prices is the *International Journal of Computational Mathematical Ideas,* an Indian journal priced at $400 per year. Volume 1, No. 3—a 61-page black-and-white paperback—is on Lulu at a remarkable $2,000, or $1,000 for download. I strongly suggest that libraries *not* emulate that pricing and note that the Lulu page does not show a sales figure, suggesting that no copies have been sold. In another case, a private publisher has 17 journals, all of which appear in print annuals from Lulu, at three-digit prices for fairly sizable volumes.

Caveats

Offering a print version of an online-only OA journal seems like a no-brainer, and in some ways it is. In particular, an annual edition, offered in both casewrap and paperback versions, would appear to be a worthwhile added outlet, serving a few libraries and authors and, if priced appropriately, bringing in a few dollars to help run the journal or the publishing program.

You do need to be aware of the limitations. An online journal can have color illustrations with no added cost; to reproduce those color illustrations in print form may be prohibitively expensive, especially if there are two color pages in a 200-page journal. Similarly, there's no real cost penalty to running very long papers online—but every page adds another 2 cents to a print edition. On balance, though, this should be an easy process and can yield good results.

13
Closing Thoughts

Your community has many stories. Some of those stories deserve to be preserved, sometimes for an immediate family, sometimes for a self-identified group, frequently for the community as a whole. Good libraries serve their communities by helping to preserve those stories.

Micropublishing offers a great way to preserve and distribute the stories in your community. The low-cost/no-cost methods discussed in this book eliminate capital investment as a bar to publication, while encouraging high-quality publications.

There's reason to believe that micropublishing and self-publishing will be increasingly important over time, as the largest traditional publishers suffer from blockbuster mentality and archaic business practices. Your library may be involved not only as a facilitator but also as a publisher of record.

Publishers Still Matter

I'm not saying publishers don't matter. They do—and there are tens of thousands of small- and medium-sized publishers that seem to care more about creating good books than moving product. The line between small publisher and self-publisher has been fuzzy for some time, and seems likely to get even fuzzier—just as the line between self-publishing and micropublishing may become more vague.

The low-cost/no-cost approach does not negate the need for good editors, copyeditors, and proofreaders. Where community resources don't suffice and where writers see the need, there's no better place to spend money than on good editing. But that's not a useful statement when you anticipate selling or distributing ten or twenty copies of a family history: The cost of professional editing alone will usually make the project untenable.

Library Roles and Community Support

This book gives your community members the tools to make the pages of a book look as good as most professionally published books, without any expense other than standard software. That's important because it fulfills a primary aim of book design and layout: getting irrelevant issues out of the way so readers focus on what's being said. Bad breaks and other design problems interfere with reading; that is reason enough to spend time avoiding them.

Your library can help with the missing part of no-cost micropublishing: getting the words right. You may have existing groups (writer's circles and the like) that can trade skills; you may find it worthwhile to build new groups. Such groups and others like them can also help critique layout, modifying the supplied templates to make individual books look more distinctive and attractive.

The next step, which will vary in each library, is what you'll do with the results. Do you collect local authors? Should you? Are there other agencies in town—local history museums, genealogy groups, what have you—that might be interested in some cases? Do you have clear guidelines on what you will and won't accept for your collection?

It should be possible to support your community's stories without promising to retain a copy of each micropublication. That will require clarity and possibly some flexibility.

Does your library already have a publishing program? If so, the tools in this book may help you publish more effectively when costs are important—and even when they're not.

If you don't, *maybe you should*—on your own or in collaboration with other agencies. That's especially true for academic libraries, where the library may be a logical place to mount a fledgling college press or keep a failing press in operation.

If your library has a local history room or collection, wouldn't it make sense to publish some specialized works about your community? With micropublishing, you can do that—even in hardcover—without major advance funding.

If your library wants to encourage teens to write and collaborate, wouldn't it be great to publish the best results? With micropublishing, it's feasible—and maybe you can even get the teens to do the work.

In academic and public libraries, working with other agencies to encourage worthwhile publications can only work to your library's credit. You'll be helping to create, organize, and preserve the records of civilization's growth—a worthy role for any library.

The Writer's Needs

This book is written for librarians, even though much of it speaks directly to writers. It's about the *why* of micropublishing and library involvement, but it's also about the *how*.

Writers and compilers preparing micropublications may need working copies of the primary "how" of this book—specifically Chapters 4, 5, and 6, and to a lesser degree Chapters 7 through 10. For the convenience of librarians, educators, and their micropublishing clienteles, Chapters 4 through 6 may be photocopied for free distribution in accordance with the "Permission to Photocopy" statement appearing on the book's copyright page.

Check this book's website, waltcrawford.name/lgm. It has links to the templates and links to resources mentioned here, and it will be the first place additional resources specifically for micropublishers are announced.

No Significant Compromise

While micropublishing inherently involves some production compromises as compared to traditional offset and letterpress bookmaking, it need not require any significant compromise for most modern books consisting primarily of text. In practice, many large-publisher books lack the page-by-page attention to typographic detail urged by this book.

The compromises are that laser-printed books may not have quite the sharpness of traditional books and that micropublishing doesn't offer the range of typeface options available from a publisher.

The first compromise, while true enough, becomes meaningless when publishers use print on demand techniques to keep books in print and put books back into print. Those print on demand books aren't going to be any sharper than the print on demand books produced through micropublishing: The production methods are identical.

The second compromise should not be a major issue. Today's best OpenType and TrueType typefaces are professionally designed and yield excellent results. For that matter, if a micropublisher wants a typeface that's not on his or her computer, individual licenses aren't terribly expensive. But for a Windows user who had Microsoft Office or Word 2007 before moving to Office 2010 and for most Macintosh OS X users, the range of first-rate typefaces should be wide enough for most books.

Customizing the Templates

The bk6pv.dotx template created for this book and provided as a downloadable file is a professional design, created by the author but improved significantly through discussions with and suggested changes from Information Today, Inc.'s vice president of graphics and production, M. Heide Dengler. ("Created by the author" may be an overstatement: I measured and analyzed the book design of a number of library-related nonfiction books in order to arrive at an initial design, which was then refined in consultation with Ms. Dengler and modified further during the production of this book.)

It's a starting point. There's no reason a micropublished book should use the template without modification. Palatino Linotype sets large, one reason this book uses 10 point type on 13 point spacing. Many other typefaces will look better with 11 point type on 13 point spacing, and for larger books, 12 point type on 14 or 15 point spacing may be a better choice. You could also consider variations of heading placement and type, with this template's levels of visible heading priority as a working example.

Which typefaces you use depends partly on what platform you're using. Almost every Windows and Macintosh computer should have Palatino (or Palatino Linotype), Verdana, Georgia, and Times New Roman. There may be other typefaces common to both platforms, including typefaces you'd be highly unlikely to use for a book (e.g., Courier New). Micropublishers should experiment, but they should check their experiments with others.

Paying Attention Page by Page

Here's where a micropublisher can do better than some large publishers: paying attention to a book's layout, paragraph by paragraph, page by page, and spread by spread. I was shocked to find that three-quarters of a random sample of contemporary books (from big publishers and university presses and all published since 2000) had bad breaks and other signs that nobody had checked each page for quality.

Chapter 6 describes methodologies that work and are nowhere near as cumbersome in practice as they may sound. As compared to real *difficulties* working with Microsoft Word layout (e.g., getting figures and captions to work exactly the way you want them, especially when you edit the text around them), fixing bad breaks and making vertical justification look good isn't difficult and doesn't take that long. (If you're a stickler for logical hyphenation, fixing hyphenation problems can take *much* longer than fixing orphan words and other bad breaks!)

Chapter 6 does not describe one final step that you should make habitual when preparing micropublications: viewing each two-page spread in Word's two-page view, to see that each spread looks right and is appropriately balanced.

Do these details matter? There's no easy answer to that question. Fixing these problems has the desirable effect of eliminating visible problems—and that encourages readers to focus on the words of a book without being distracted by layout problems.

Passing It On

One good reason to publish a few casewrap (hardcover) copies of a micropublished book is that casewrap books seem more substantial to people, making it more likely that they'll be kept for a longer time and, as appropriate, passed along to the next generation. (As mentioned before, for proof of concept, see the hardcover edition of this book available through Lulu.)

If a micropublisher is writing a family history or telling family stories, passing it on can involve not only producing casewrap copies but also freeing future generations to build on the current work by using a Creative Commons license to explicitly allow such reuse. Micropublishers have one thing in common with scholars writing journal articles: They should be more concerned with having their work read and used than with the restrictions of copyright.

Other Libraries

This book focuses on public libraries and, to a lesser extent, academic libraries. What about school libraries and special libraries?

School and special libraries can certainly use micropublishing techniques to become publishers, if there are appropriate needs. Special libraries may have patrons who would use micropublishing techniques if they knew about them. As for patrons of school libraries, if they're in a position to handle contractual issues involved in micropublishing (and receiving revenues) or if they have the support of parents or guardians, they might also be potential micropublishers.

Every library has or should have the creation and gathering of new knowledge as part of its mission. These days, digital techniques may account for most of that creation and gathering—but sometimes, a book is one desirable outcome. Where a book makes sense but the market is very small, micropublishing is the solution.

Starting Small

The great thing about micropublishing is that you *can* start small without blocking later growth. When members of your community find that their little book of local lore has a much larger potential audience than they envisioned, you can help them move beyond micropublishing. When you identify new needs for publications, you can help those publications emerge. You may even be able to gain a little funding for the library: There's nothing that says micropublications have to be sold at cost.

Micropublishing offers a growing range of possibilities for libraries of all sorts. I hope you'll find this book useful in exploring those possibilities.

Glossary

Back Matter. Sections of a book that follow the final chapter, including afterword, appendices, endnotes, glossary, bibliography, about the author, and index.

Bad Break. A bad break is typically defined as a hyphenation problem, such as the last word of a paragraph broken over a line, a contraction broken over a line, a word broken across pages, or a word that's broken over a line so that only two letters appear before or after the hyphen. This book uses bad breaks in a broader sense, to include orphan words, cases where a short word or part of a word is the last line of a multiline paragraph. Where feasible, bad breaks should be prevented. Microsoft Word does not have automatic tools to do this, but condensing or expanding spacing within a paragraph by a nearly invisible amount can correct bad breaks of all sorts.

Cascading Styles. Styles that inherit some of their characteristics from parent styles (e.g., in the template used for this book, Heading 2, Heading 3, and Heading 4 are all children of Heading 1, so that a change to the Heading 1 typeface will cascade to the other three styles).

Casewrap. The kind of hardcover book you're most likely to get at Lulu, if you're willing to pay the substantial extra price. A casewrap book, in Lulu's case, has the cover design printed directly on the hard binding, with the pages glued to a cloth strip within the binding.

Character Spacing. Uniform spacing between letters within a word, line, sentence, or paragraph, as implemented in Word's **Font** dialog box (the **Advanced** tab). Expanded spacing might be used for special effects in headings. Condensed and expanded spacing at the lowest settings (0.1 or 0.2 points) are useful to eliminate bad breaks. Both can be used to clean up interparagraph spacing problems when using vertical justification.

Colophon. A brief description of production notes for a book, generally including typefaces used and sometimes including software used and who was responsible for specific production steps. The colophon may appear on the copyright (back-of-title) page or as its own page in either front or back matter.

Copyediting. Detailed editing, checking for grammar, punctuation, and consistency in spelling, capitalization, and stylistic elements. In fiction, a copyeditor ensures that character names have been used consistently. Some copyeditors also question factual issues and raise warning flags on possible libel or copyright infringement.

Copyfitting. Touching up a document so that it fits the page as well as possible. I use it here mostly to refer to the process of correcting bad breaks by expanding or condensing paragraphs.

Copyright. The exclusive legal right to reproduce, publish, sell, or distribute a creative work, such as a book, song, blog post, or play. Your book is protected by copyright as soon as you print out the text or store it to hard disk, unless you explicitly place your book in the public domain. Copyright *registration* is required to sue for infringement and obtain statutory damages, but it is not necessary for most micropublications.

CreateSpace. One of two major publish on demand service providers that lets you prepare books and make them available for sale with no up-front costs (except one required proof copy, and that requirement may be changing). CreateSpace is a division of Amazon that also supports creation and distribution of CDs, DVDs, downloadable music and video content, and Kindle ebooks (but not other ebook formats, PDF downloads, or hardcover books).

Creative Commons. A nonprofit organization that develops and supports licenses that allow you to explicitly waive some aspects of copyright protection. A CC BY license, for example, explicitly says that someone else can copy your text and develop other text based on it—as long as you're credited as the originator of the text (the BY portion), while BY-NC, perhaps the most common license, also requires that the copies distributed be non-commercial in nature.

DRM. Digital Rights Management. Broadly, DRM includes all tools to manage people's rights to use digital material. Narrowly, DRM includes copy protection and the like.

Font. Although frequently used as synonymous with typeface, a font is technically one size and style of a typeface. So, for example, this text uses two fonts: 10 point Palatino Linotype normal and 10 point Palatino Linotype bold. Long quoted material within this book uses the same typeface as headings—Verdana—but a different font, 10 point Verdana normal.

Front Matter. Sections of a book that precede the first chapter, typically including title page, copyright page, table of contents, and sometimes half-title page, dedication, acknowledgments, foreword, preface, and introduction; some blank pages are required to ensure that most of these sections (except the copyright page) and the first chapter all begin on right-hand (recto) pages.

ISBN. International Standard Book Number. A 13-digit number that typically appears with a bar code on the back cover of a book. Books sold in retail bookstores usually (but not always) require ISBNs, as do books intended for listing in *Books in Print*. Books sold entirely through Lulu do not require ISBNs. While obtaining your own ISBN that identifies your own imprint is expensive (starting at $125 in the U.S.), both Lulu and CreateSpace will assign ISBNs to your books for free, although those ISBNs can only be used with the Lulu or CreateSpace editions and identify the service provider as the publisher of record.

Justification. The lining up of text with the left, center, right, or both margins. Most commonly, and in this book, "justified" is used to mean fully justified, that is, with the text lining up on both left and right margins (except for the last line of each paragraph). I use "left aligned," "centered," and "right aligned" for the other three options.

Kerning. Adjusting the spacing of pairs of characters so they're more visually pleasing and, in turn, more readable. Word supports kerning once you enable it, and kerning pairs are defined in most good typefaces. "AV" and "Yo" are examples of kerning.

Layout. For micropublishing, the look of a book's text pages, also called *page layout*: Margins, nature of headings and space above and below headings, type size and line spacing, special features if any. The layout for a book prepared using Word may be represented and enforced by its template.

Leading. Space between lines of a paragraph, expressed either as a percentage (e.g., 20 percent leading) or as a point count—typically but not always combining the space between lines and the line height in points. So, for example, you could say that this book uses 30 percent leading, as it adds 3 points of space to the 10 point text. Word uses the less ambiguous *line spacing* instead.

Legibility. Ease of recognizing the characters on a page (or on a screen). Distinctly different from *readability*.

LibreOffice. An open source, freely downloadable office suite, currently identical to OpenOffice. Capable of producing high-quality results, but with somewhat less flexibility and more cumbersome processes than Microsoft Office and Word.

Ligatures. Combinations of two letters such as ff or fi (or, in cases as shown here, st and sp) and, sometimes, special forms of letters at different points in a word. While Word 2010 enables ligatures (not by default), very few supplied typefaces support them. Unless you're preparing an unusual book (e.g., a family story that's supposed to have the elegance of age) you probably won't worry about ligatures. (Palatino Linotype as supplied with Windows 7 has extensive ligature support. For this definition, all ligatures and special forms were enabled.) Note that expanding or condensing type will frequently break ligatures.

Line Editing. Substantive editing, sometimes just called editing, where the editor suggests or requires revisions to a manuscript that may be as small as changing a particular word or as large as completely removing or moving chapters.

Line Spacing. The space in points from the base of one line of type to the base of the next line of type. This book uses 13 point line spacing, fairly typical for 11 point type (since line spacing is usually about 20 percent larger than type) and used here for 10 point type because Palatino Linotype "sets large," that is, has taller characters than most 10 point type.

Lulu. One of two major publish on demand service providers, a company that lets you prepare books and make them available for sale with no up-front costs. Lulu is an independent company that labels its business as "Self publishing and printing solutions" and also supports creation of calendars, CDs, DVDs, and ebooks. Lulu supports creation of hardcover books and PDF downloads, and supports other ebook formats as well.

Micropublishing. Using print on demand fulfillment services to publish books that may serve niches from one to 500 copies, by producing books individually as they are needed.

Office. Used as an informal abbreviation for Microsoft Office, most commonly Office 2010 in this book.

Orphan. Either the first line of a multiline paragraph appearing stranded at the bottom of a page, or the last line of a paragraph consisting of a partial word or a short single word.

Outsourcing. Hiring others to handle some of the steps in publishing a book, such as line editing, copyediting, or cover design. Technically, when you use Lulu or CreateSpace, you're outsourcing printing and fulfillment.

PDF. Portable Document Format. The standard format to upload books for Lulu and CreateSpace, developed and maintained by Adobe Corporation.

PDF/A. The standardized archival version of PDF, which embeds all typefaces (meeting Lulu and CreateSpace upload requirements) but produces substantially larger files than Adobe Acrobat set to embed all typefaces. Office 2010 and LibreOffice can both generate PDF/A files directly.

Perfect-Bound. The binding on nearly all Lulu and CreateSpace books (Lulu offers other forms of binding in special cases). For micropublished books, perfect binding means that individual sheets are glued into a heavy paper cover.

Pica. One-sixth of an inch. A standard measure in typography. Usually abbreviated p. This book has a text block that's 26 picas wide and 42 picas (and 3 points) tall, on a page that's 36 by 54 picas (that is, a 6" x 9" page, the most common U.S. size for trade paperbacks and hardbound books).

POD. Formally, *print on demand*. Producing books one at a time as they are ordered. Informally, *publish on demand*.

Point. One-twelfth of a pica or one-72nd of an inch. Typically abbreviated pt. The standard measure for type size and line spacing. The exact size of a point has varied over time, but since desktop publishing became common, it's been fixed at one-72nd of an inch.

Print on Demand. One-off book production, typically producing books only as they are ordered, using high-speed laser printers and separate cover printers. Print on Demand can be done via in-house book production systems such as the Espresso Book Machine or offsite through dedicated print on demand suppliers such as Lightning Source and BookSurge. Many publishers use print on demand suppliers to keep older books in print by producing very small quantities to fill anticipated demand.

Proofreading. Making sure words are spelled correctly and are the intended words (for example, that "there" hasn't been used where "their" or "they're" was intended). Proofreading deals only with accuracy, not writing quality.

Publish on Demand. Informal term used to describe the process done by Lulu, CreateSpace, and possibly others. These services list books for sale, take orders, produce books only as sold, and ship those books to customers, providing complete fulfillment functions for micropublishers.

Readability. Ease of *reading* a collection of words as comprehensible sentences and paragraphs. Serif text (such as the body text used in this book) has generally been found to be more readable than sans serif text (such as that used for headings in this book), partly because the serifs help to connect letters into words.

Recto. The right-hand page or front of each sheet of paper in a book, normally with an odd page number.

Sans Serif. Typeface that lacks serifs, such as Verdana. Many modern book designs, including the one used for this book and its template, use a sans serif typeface for headings that complements the serif typeface used for body text.

Self-Publishing. Publishing your own books under your own name or an imprint you create, as opposed to working with a publisher. Almost all micropublishing is also self-publishing, but (in terms of book sales) most self-publishing is not micropublishing. Traditional self-publishing involves thousands of dollars of up-front costs and traditional book production methods.

Serif. The little crosslines (e.g., the two little vertical lines at the top of "T") that differentiate serif typefaces from sans serif typefaces. Most American designers, and decades of readability studies, regard serif typefaces as more readable for long printed text.

Styles. The names and definitions of paragraph and heading types in Word, such as Normal, First, Heading 1, and Quote1. When headings and paragraphs are tagged as and defined by styles, rather than modifying paragraph typeface and placement directly, they can be kept consistent and altered uniformly throughout a document.

Template. For Word, a template is a document from which you build other documents. It primarily contains definitions for styles used within a document but also defines page size and can include example text and other elements.

Typography. Generally, the art and technique of arranging type. Closely related to and overlapping with layout. This can include selecting typefaces, selecting point sizes and line spacing, and using kerning and other techniques to make text look better and be more readable.

Vanity Press. A publisher that requires the author to pay up-front costs but publishes books under the vanity press's name. Those costs may be hidden as requirements for the author to purchase a minimum number of copies or may be stated in other ways. A true publish on demand service may offer additional priced services but will not *require* any author subsidization or claim to be a publisher.

Verso. The left-hand page or back of each sheet of paper in a book, normally with an even page number.

Vertical Justification. Adding space between paragraphs within a page or column of text so that columns and pages always begin and end at the same point. Word has the unfortunate bad habit of attempting to justify the last page of a chapter. Sometimes called feathering.

Widow. The last line of a multiline paragraph that appears by itself at the top of a page. Word will automatically prevent widows unless you tell it not to.

Word. Used as an informal abbreviation for Microsoft Word. While this book uses Microsoft Word 2010 for all examples, most techniques described should work equally well in Word 2007 and possibly older versions, as well as related versions for Macintosh.

Bibliography

Appelbaum, Judith. *How to Get Happily Published* (Fourth edition). New York: HarperPerennial, 1992.

For micropublishing, this book serves best as a source of advice on publicity and marketing, and also offers resources on writing and editing. A more recent edition (1998) is available.

Brownstone, David M. and Irene M. Franck. *The Complete Self-Publishing Handbook* (New Revised Edition). New York: Plume, 1999.

The first edition of this book, in 1985, had the title *The Self-Publishing Handbook*. This book is priced like a trade paperback ($13.95 in 1999 dollars) but looks like a mass-market paperback (5.2" x 8" and printed on cheap paper that's already yellowing pretty badly). It includes a fair amount of decent advice and some not-so-great advice; it's good on marketing and offers some shockingly high but probably realistic numbers for the costs of self-publishing. One of the calmer and better-edited books on self-publishing; notably not self-published.

Corson-Finnerty, Adam. "Micro-Publishing," March 9, 2009 post on *Musings of Mine*. musingsofcorsonf.blogspot.com/2009/03/micro-publishing.html

Corson-Finnerty discusses Penn Libraries' use of the Espresso Book Machine, a self-contained on-site print on demand system, and experience with the machine at the University of Alberta's bookstore. The University of Alberta found (to its surprise) that author-originated books dominated use of the machine, in essence an even more distributed case of micropublishing. Corson-Finnerty notes such possibilities as books designed for one class of 30 people that are still profitable and books created by combining articles in a database. A key quote from the University of Alberta experience: "It's amazing what perfect binding can do for an author."

Ivins, October and Judy Luther. *Publishing Support for Small Print-Based Publishers: Options for ARL Libraries.* February 2011. Available for download at www.arl.org/sc/models/pub-support.

This free report provides valuable examples and insights into academic libraries as publishers and libraries supporting scholarly publishing. It's primarily concerned with journals but covers other areas as well.

Judd, Karen. *Copyediting: A Practical Guide.* Los Altos, California: William Kaufmann, Inc., 1982.

Although portions of this book are seriously dated, the core discussions of what copyediting is and why it matters continue to be useful.

Poynter, Dan, *Dan Poynter's Self-Publishing Manual* (Sixteenth Edition). Santa Barbara: Para Publishing, 2007.

Poynter is well known in self-publishing circles, and this manual frequently urges you to buy other Para books and special reports. I find Poynter's style annoying and repetitive, but he's very strong on self-promotion and book promotion. Indeed, Poynter seems to regard establishing a market for a book as more important than actually writing the book. He also seems to loathe traditional publishers for changing the precious words of writers. I've generally found that good publishers offer editorial suggestions that improve my prose, so I'm not inclined to agree (and I believe Poynter would benefit from good editing).

His list of POD publishers wholly omits Lulu and CreateSpace, both of which were well established by 2007. He lumps POD providers he *does* include (e.g., AuthorHouse) in with vanity presses, and he may be right.

Traditional self-publishing is almost necessarily mostly about marketing, and the numbers show why: Using Poynter's advice, you're in for $10,000 or more initial investment—and 300 copies of your book will be gone before you sell the first one. If you want to sell thousands of copies of a book, Poynter may have useful advice, even though I found his style and approach unpalatable.

Radke, Linda Foster. *The Economical Guide to Self-Publishing: How to Produce and Market Your Book on a Budget.* Chandler, AZ: Five Star Publications, 1996.

Radke offers advice on marketing and production, but this self-published book (at least in the 1996 edition) is an example of the problems with much self-publishing. I see no real evidence of advice leading to economies.

Sander, Jennifer Basye. *The Complete Idiot's Guide to Self-Publishing.* New York: Alpha, 2005.

This book is filled with good advice on marketing and some of the *real* costs of hiring things out. Unfortunately, Sander assumes that iUniverse and AuthorHouse are self-publishers and never mentions Lulu, so the line between self-publishing and vanity press is fuzzier than usual (since iUniverse and AuthorHouse charge up-front fees). She's also given to absolute statements that probably didn't make sense in 2005 and certainly don't in 2011 (e.g., never use TrueType, never use Microsoft Word for formatting) or ignorant of established fact (she questions the longevity of POD because it's laser toner on paper—but the archival lifespan of properly applied laser toner on acid-free paper is well established). Otherwise, I like this one: some frank (even brutal) advice on your chances and lots of ways to get your book noticed.

Strauss, Victoria. "Lies (Dishonest) Fee-Charging Publishers Tell." Posted April 4, 2011 at *Writer Beware™ Blogs!*: accrispin.blogspot.com/2011/04/lies-dishonest-fee-charging-publishers.html.

Writer Beware™ Blogs! is a prime source for information and commentary on vanity presses and "the shadow-world of literary scams, schemes, and pitfalls." This post examines a number of ways that vanity publishers attempt to evade that label. Well worth reading (as is the blog and the site in general).

About the Author

Walt Crawford is a retired library systems analyst/programmer who writes and occasionally speaks on libraries, technology, policy, and media. From October 2007 through March 2010, Crawford was editorial director of the Library Leadership Network. For almost 30 years before that, he was a senior analyst at RLG, focusing on user interface design and actual usage patterns for end-user bibliographic search systems.

Crawford's books include *Open Access: What You Need to Know Now* (2011), *First Have Something to Say: Writing for the Library Profession* (2003), and thirteen others going back to *MARC for Library Use: Understanding the USMARC Formats* (1984). He has also micropublished several books including *Library 2.0: A Cites & Insights Reader* (2011), *Open Access and Libraries: Essays from Cites & Insights 2001–2009* (2010), and other titles going back to *Balanced Libraries: Thoughts on Continuity and Change* (2007), including a series on library blogs and librarian blogs.

Crawford has written columns for *American Libraries, EContent, ONLINE Magazine,* and *Library Hi Tech.* In 1995, he received the American Library Association's LITA/Library Hi Tech Award for Excellence in Communication for Continuing Education, followed by the ALCTS/Blackwell Scholarship Award in 1997. He was president of the Library and Information Technology Association in 1992/93.

Index

More Great Books from Information Today, Inc.

The Cybrarian's Web
An A–Z Guide to 101 Free Web 2.0 Tools and Other Resources

By Cheryl Ann Peltier-Davis

Here is a remarkable field guide to the best free Web 2.0 tools and their practical applications in libraries and information centers. Designed for info pros who want to use the latest tech tools to connect, collaborate, and create, you'll find resources to help you build a customized social network, start an ebook lending program, publicize events and innovations, and more! You'll discover dozens of lesser-known resources and learn exciting new ways to use many of the most popular sites and tools. With all this and a supporting webpage, *The Cybrarian's Web* is a winner!

512 pp/softbound/ISBN 978-1-57387-427-4 $49.50

The Librarian's Guide to Negotiation
Winning Strategies for the Digital Age

By Beth Ashmore, Jill E. Grogg, and Jeff Weddle

Librarians negotiate every day with vendors, funding agencies, administrators, employees, co-workers, and patrons—yet the art of negotiation receives little attention in library education and training. This practical guide by three experienced librarian-negotiators will help you develop the mindset, skills, and confidence you need to negotiate effectively in any situation. The authors provide an in-depth look at negotiation in theory and practice, share tactics and strategies of top negotiators, offer techniques for overcoming emotional responses to conflict, recall successful outcomes and deals gone awry, and demonstrate the importance of negotiating expertise to libraries and library careers. The result is an eye-opening survey into the true nature of negotiation—both as a form of communication and as a tool you can use to create sustainable collections and improve library service in the digital age.

264 pp/softbound/ISBN 978-1-57387-428-1 $49.50

Implementing Technology Solutions in Libraries
Techniques, Tools, and Tips From the Trenches

By Karen C. Knox

For anyone seeking a straightforward, hands-on approach to implementing technology solutions in libraries, this is your guide! Created for staff who want to ensure success with a technology project that may consume a significant part of the library's budget, author and IT manager Karen Knox deconstructs an entire project implementation, from planning to evaluation, carefully examining each step. She draws on her experience to help readers identify the most critical components of any project while modifying and scaling to meet their library's unique needs. The array of tips, tricks, techniques, and tools she shares here are designed to spell success in your next library technology implementation.

192 pp/softbound/ISBN 978-1-57387-403-8 $35.00

UContent
The Information Professional's Guide to User-Generated Content

By Nicholas G. Tomaiuolo

Have you ever reviewed a book at Amazon.com? Uploaded a photo to Flickr? Commented on a blog posting? Used tags to describe or access information? If you have, you've contributed user-generated content (UContent) to the web. But while many librarians and information professionals have accepted their roles as creators and managers of UContent, many have not. This comprehensive text considers the reasons behind UContent's wild popularity and makes strong arguments for cultivating it. While describing his own UContent experiences, the author has prepared a well researched book that serves as an overview, a status report, a primer, and a prognostication.

360 pp/softbound/ISBN 978-1-57387-425-0 $49.50